D1569650

In
Defense
of

. . . .

MODERNITY

. . . .

In
Defense
of
MODERNITY

Role Complexity
and
Individual Autonomy

ROSE LAUB COSER

STANFORD UNIVERSITY PRESS
Stanford, California
1991

Stanford University Press
Stanford, California
©1991 by the Board of Trustees of the
Leland Stanford Junior University
Printed in the United States of America

CIP data appear at the end of the book

For Bob

Acknowledgments

This book was long in the making. Teaching, research other than for this book, committee obligations, and some feminist militancy and personal obligations—a complex agenda indeed—left much of the writing for time off. The book was begun in 1980 at the Center for Advanced Study in the Behavioral Sciences at Stanford University with the help of a grant from the John Simon Guggenheim Memorial Foundation. A year at the Ecole des Hautes Etudes in Paris provided another good stretch of time, and finally the years after my retirement in 1986 made the completion of the book possible.

My thanks go to the staff of the Center for Advanced Study in the Behavioral Sciences and its then director, Gardner Lindzey; to Clemens Heller of La Maison des Sciences de l'Homme in Paris; and to the Henry A. Murray Center of Radcliffe College and its staff, scholars, and director, Anne Colby, for providing not only affiliation but office space and especially colleagueship.

Many colleagues have contributed to this book. Robert K. Merton has taught me sociology and has provided the theoretical framework. Lewis Coser has listened, has read and reread, and with his theoretical acumen has offered comments and criticism—not tiring of many hours of discussions—and, not to forget, his patience. Mark Granovetter and Gerald Platt have offered extensive comments. The book has also profited from a careful reading by Sanford Dornbusch and the anonymous reader for Stanford University Press. Muriel Bell and Gladys Topkis have helped with editorial comments, and Julia Johnson Zafferano has shown utmost skill and sensitivity in the editing of my manuscript.

Over all these years I have had the advantage of conversations with many colleagues, mainly at the State University of New York at Stony Brook and also lately at Boston College. They are too many to be enumerated here. I only want to mention that years of colleagueship and friendship with Gladys Rothbell gave me the opportunity to try out many of my ideas. For many years Norman Goodman and lately John Williamson, William Gamson, and Paul Gray were generous in their support.

Lila Czelowalnik has shown extreme patience and skill in typing and retyping the manuscript with the thought and care such an endeavor demands, and often beyond the call of duty. The administrative staff at Boston College—Eunice Doherty, Mary McMillan, Roberta Nerenberg, Shirley Urban, and Barbara Smith—have been most cooperative in complying with almost daily requests. My thanks go to them all as well as to Patricia O'Grady, my able assistant during the last hurdle.

R. L. C.

Contents

In
Defense
of

MODERNITY

The rank order of the primates was one-dimensional: every individual could occupy one and only one—that is, in all functional domains the same—status. Only when the same individual could unify various status positions and different individuals could occupy the same status was a socially regulated exchange between functionally specified subsystems possible.

—Jürgen Habermas,
Communication and the Evolution of Society

I argue that the higher intellectual faculties . . . have evolved as an adaptation to the complexities of social living.

—N. K. Humphrey,
"The Social Function of Intellect"

Introduction

P eople develop a notion of who and what they are in interaction with others, a process in which confirmation is sought and modification is achieved step by step. This process is smoothest where interactors know one another well enough to take one another for granted. At the other extreme, where interactors are complete strangers to one another, the encounter is awkward because there is no common ground for definition of self and others. The usual chit-chat that takes place on such occasions, typically after an exchange of formalities, attests to the absence of what Max Weber (1947a) called a shared definition of the relationship, which would enable the interactors to help one another in defining their various roles.

Between these extreme situations are those in which individuals know something about the people they meet, such as their positions in the social structure, if only in a superficial way. Social positions indicate some general attributes these persons want to convey. If I meet a department head for the first time, I know that this person wants to convey an image of efficiency and control. If I meet my child's teacher, I know that he or she wants to convey concern for students, pedagogic astuteness, and some acquaintance with subject matter in addition to an image of control.

Every series of encounters that involve moving from one

sphere of activity to another and dealing with different people in each sphere requires individuals to articulate their roles more self-consciously than if they remain within a stable group where they are known in their whole being and know the other members in the same way. As compared to a segmented activity, one that is not known in one's other relationships, a group in which one's predispositions and attitudes are well known to all, as in the family or among friends, is experienced as psychologically restful— as a place where you can "put your feet up" and "let your hair down"— that is, where you do not have to adjust your "face" (Goffman 1955). An invitation to "make yourself at home" is meant to convey that one need not bother defining and presenting segments of oneself or remaining at attention for the purpose of exchanging cues with people only partially known.

Although in all societies people work to ensure their subsistence, live in families, socialize the young and one another, and fill public roles that serve political, religious, health, educational, and ceremonial purposes, only in modern industrial society is work usually separated from the home in time and place. This has not only introduced a high level of rationality into the productive process (Henderson and Parsons 1947; Weber 1978) but also produced a fundamental change in all aspects of everyday life. At work away from home, people behave with only some segments of their personality. At home, in contrast, family members in general participate more or less with their total personality, although in recent decades even the family has become the locus of increasingly segmented relationships. This is because, when everyone is away at work or school all day, even family members have to become acquainted on nights and weekends with one another's preoccupations.

In modern society, social roles usually cannot be taken for granted but must be negotiated even if everyone has a general conception of what it means to be a mother or father, physician or teacher. Even this becomes more and more uncertain, as the proliferation of uncounted and infinitely various types of therapy seems to testify.

Where relationships are segmented and people move in time

and space from one activity to another, they are forced to articulate their roles; that is, they have to figure out or recall the type of behavior appropriate for the occasion. If they fall short of what is expected, they will be cued in by their partners in the interaction. This is what I meant in my opening sentence: confirmation of who one is and how one may or should behave is constantly sought, and modification is more or less constantly achieved (T. Parsons 1951: 3–22).

Social roles were not invented by sociologists. They merely systematized the use of the concept. The idea of social roles is implicit in everyday language, in the words that denote a person's position in relation to that of other people. If we call someone a teacher, we imply not only that this person occupies a position entailing specific demands and rewards (status) and that the person teaches (task), but also that in doing so he or she relates to students (role). If we identify someone as mother, we mean not only that this woman engages in parenting and caring activities but also that she does so in relation to one or several children who are acknowledged to be hers. Implicit in the denotation of people is usually the connotation of their relationships within the social structure. This is why social role does not necessarily refer to specific and unalterable behavior (for example, writing on the blackboard for a teacher) but expresses one or several relationships sustained by a repertory of behaviors (R. Coser 1966). Interactions and the norms that govern them are both fostered and controlled by shared knowledge and mutual conveyance of the participants' specific positions in the social structure. The department head and school teacher mentioned above are identified by their social positions, by the words I use to identify them. Knowledge of these positions, I said, provides guidelines for other parties in the interaction. From such knowledge a consensus develops about the social roles that exist in one's environment and the range of behaviors appropriate to them. This is not so clear-cut, of course, in traditional rural society, where a woman's husband is also the farmer and often an entrepreneur, and where people in the community are usually known to one another. One does not need to identify people by their positions if all are known to all.

Explicitness in identification by status goes together with explicitness in role articulation. This process can be best illustrated by examples from somewhat unusual situations. If one has to move into an unfamiliar social setting, such as a hospital, it takes time and deliberate effort to get one's bearings, to locate one's own status in relation to those of other people. This is, at least in part, what is meant by "making an adjustment." It is worth noting that the term "adjustment" has acquired increasing importance in modern society. In the old-time rural village, the notion was probably not as salient, if it existed at all, as it is in present-day urban society. The measure of adjustment needed in a situation correlates with the explicitness needed for *status identification* and with the individual's need for *role articulation*.

Transitional Status and Sociological Ambivalence

The relative lack of overlap between social groups in modern society accounts in at least a small way for the experience psychologists call *separation anxiety*. The separation is not merely from what these psychologists call a love object—that is, from a person to whom one is affectively attached. Separation from a social setting means separation from a whole set of role partners; it means a loosening if not a loss of relationships in that setting. Whether or not one is affectively attached to one's role partners, separation from them means the loss of people who have helped define and articulate one's role through regular interaction. Typically, such departures are punctuated by ceremonies, ranging in formality from farewell parties to commencement exercises—formalities that help ease the social anxiety that comes with *transitional status*.

Separation anxiety is most acutely felt by youngsters starting school for the first time, leaving one school for another, or leaving school altogether, or by adults who change jobs or training sites. In these patterned social situations, individuals find themselves in transitional statuses. The so-called problems of adolescence include the important process of change in role partners. Although not all transitional statuses are given formal recognition, they are informally identified by such expressions as "lame duck"—someone whose status of some importance is about to come to an end—or "greenhorn"—someone who is not yet quite recognized in a status that is in the process of being acquired. Even preparing to leave one's abode for a holiday trip, an experience that is socially expected to call forth happy anticipation, creates anxiety regarding the unknown (an emotion for which the German language has the term *Reisefieber*).

It should be clear, then, that separation anxiety is likely to have its source in the social structure, one that is segmented into the familiar and the unfamiliar. Anxiety arises where there is an expected loss of relationships that used to help confirm who one is, to be replaced by a set of relationships yet unknown where status articulation has to take place anew.

This helps us understand the acute anxiety of children when they start school or when they are taken to a strange environment, like a hospital. In addition to the traumatic experience of the loss of affective ties, they find themselves in an environmental vacuum, one that translates into an emotional vacuum. If it is difficult for adults to articulate their roles where all role partners are strangers and their social positions are unfamiliar, it is well-nigh impossible for children who are not yet able to separate feelings from cognition. Policies that permit a parent to stay with a child in the hospital, or the policy of some progressive nursery schools that allows or even requires the parent to stay in the classroom for a while after school has begun, provide social remedies for such discontinuities in the child's world.

As another example, imagine the boy in juvenile court who hears his own lawyer say to the attorney for the prosecution "I'll see you Sunday at the squash court." Not able to understand that his defense attorney is on his side in only one social role—as the boy's lawyer—and that in another social role he or she is the other attorney's colleague, the youngster feels betrayed and confused—a feeling that is difficult for him to articulate. His emotions are likely to engulf his cognitive assessment of the situation. This may encourage diffuse acting out and ultimately lead such a youngster to seek comfortable refuge in a group or gang where the other members are predictable or where he can be predictable to himself.

The social patterns that can help individuals to make the transition from one status to another—rites of passage or other ceremonies, and even rules of etiquette—are not available for all situations of status passage. Two examples from Erving Goffman's paper "Role Distance" (1961) illustrate this point.

In his detailed description of the behavior of children of different ages on a merry-go-round, Goffman notes that at age seven or eight boys dissociate themselves "from the kind of horseman a merry-go-round allows [them] to be. . . . [They] test limits . . . and show distance by handling the task with bored, nonchalant competence, a candy bar languidly held in one hand" (p. 108). However, to Goffman's astute observations one should add that these boys are not expected by the older boys to enjoy such kid stuff; the youngsters' clowning is a display of superior status (P. Blau 1964: 40), but at the same time they are not yet granted the claim to such higher status.

Another of Goffman's examples is that of "six lower-middle-class high school girls taking a vacation in a national park and deciding to 'do' horseback riding on one of their mornings" (p. 111). These girls, it turns out, showed that they did not take horseback riding seriously, since they fooled around, clowning and mocking both horses and themselves.

If we realize that the girls wanted to show one another that they did not want to pretend to engage in an upper-middle-class activity—a claim they would not grant one another—it seems clear that in Goffman's illustrations the actors wanted to show that they could belong to a higher-status group, yet they were not free to make this claim in the presence of the group to which they belonged. These are typical cases of *sociological ambivalence* (R. Coser 1966; Merton and Barber 1976). According to Robert Merton and Elinor Barber, sociological ambivalence "refers to incompatible normative expectations of attitudes, beliefs, and behavior assigned to a status or to a set of statuses" (p. 6). A typical sociologically ambivalent situation arises when role partners of different statuses, and with whom relationships differ, are unexpectedly present at the same time; for example, if graduate students having a bull session are suddenly "intruded upon" by a faculty member. There will be a sudden embarrassed silence and, typically, some joking in response to what is experienced as a disturbance.

The use of humor is indeed a much-approved mechanism for alleviating or, better still, denying ambiguity, as I have shown elsewhere (R. Coser 1960). It is not surprising that a sense of humor is a much-appreciated quality in members of bureaucratic organizations, which have multiple and frequently incompatible status positions.

The Learning of Social Roles

Role segmentation has to be learned. The process of becoming social is not merely one of learning the do's and don'ts involved in conforming to adult role expectations. Socialization refers to the progressive development in the understanding of interpersonal relationships.

Young children have problems with role segmentation because they cannot assimilate in their scheme of comprehension all the role partners they encounter. As I have argued elsewhere (1975a), the development of mental abilities takes place together with the progressive grasp of the complexity of social relations. That intellectual comprehension should be in large measure an attribute of the social structure seems at first to be a daring assertion. Yet it should not be surprising that people who have to deal with many others in different positions, each of whom may have a different vantage point, are forced to reflect upon and take account of these other perspectives when making decisions about their own actions or about the behavior of others. The various intentions of others have to be gauged, and one's own actions have to be adapted to one's expectations of the different ways in which these others are going to behave.

Socialization in modern middle-class society consists largely in helping develop the ability to make this mental effort. It differs from socialization in simpler societies in that it requires increased differentiation of thought and action. Understanding others— that is, imagining oneself in the position of others—is the essence of social interaction. To do so successfully means that one is able to differentiate between self and others and, more important, between the others who stand in mutual relationships. Increasing differentiation is the process by which the mind develops through childhood and adolescence to what is loosely called maturity. From the point at which a baby discovers the difference between itself and its mother (generally between six and eight months), becomes aware of the threat of abandonment (Spitz and Wolf 1946), learns the difference between the rattle and its arm, and gains a sense of mastery as it now picks up the object and drops it deliberately and repeatedly and causes it to make the familiar noise, all the while chuckling with pleasure at the discovery of its own power, to the development of the sense of "I" (Mead 1946) and the later ability to deal with advanced mathematics, there is a steady increase in a person's mental ability to differentiate first between self and others, and then between an increasing number of variables, symbols, and persons as they relate to one another.

The small child showing a picture to a person facing her keeps the picture turned toward herself because she does not know the difference between her own position and that of her partner. Once she knows that the picture has to be turned around so as to be seen from the other side, the child has made a big step in social development. Socialization consists largely in acquiring the ability to put oneself in the position of others while keeping one's own position in mind. Lawrence Kohlberg and Carol Gilligan (1972: 155) quote a child who describes this process: "You have to like dream that your mind leaves your body and goes into the other person, then it comes back into you and you see it like he does and you act like the way you saw it from there."

The image of the ball game used by George Herbert Mead (1946: 151) is useful here. The individual "must be ready to take the attitude of everyone else involved in that game" and relate the players to one another; the individual "must know what everyone else is going to do in order to carry out his play" and organize into a sort of unit the attitudes of the other players. The decision as to what behavior to select for effective action will be made in relation to the *different positions* of the players in relation to one another. That is, not only must the child take the attitude of everyone else involved in the game in relation to himself, but he must be able to take the attitude of all others in relation to one another. The child must learn not only to *reverse* the roles but also to *relate* them. Reversibility is a necessary but not sufficient condition for acquiring a sense of relativity.

This ability should not be taken for granted, nor should its importance be underestimated. We are all familiar with the small child who, for example, invites the mail carrier into the house to "come have some of the cookies Mommy baked today." We laugh and find this cute, but we would react quite differently if an older child, who "should know better" behaved in this way. Knowing better means knowing that the mail carrier relates differently to the family than its own members relate to one another.

Everyone who has children or younger siblings knows that small children have some difficulty understanding that mother is not father's mother as well as their own. Not before the age of seven or eight, and sometimes even later, are children fully able to understand that someone relates in a particular way. They universalize their own relationships because they cannot yet differentiate them from others outside themselves. For them, motherhood is absolute, pertaining to the person, not to the relationship. They cannot yet conceive of the relationship between mother and father as being independent of themselves. At this age children are not able to relate to each other two variables outside of themselves— for example, volume and weight, in order to understand why a boat does not sink.*

Seeing things in perspective depends on that same ability. The small child's graphic presentation of a table is a rectangle and four perpendicular lines. This is not the table *as we see it.* In the young imagination the table is related to the self rather than to the framework of walls in the room. The table cannot be drawn in perspective before the child has reached the stage of mental development at which the outlines can be related to the surrounding walls.

To see things in perspective is to see things *relatively.* The abil-

* I am sure it is clear to the knowledgeable reader that my description of a child's conceptual development of social relations is based on the theory of Jean Piaget. See especially his *Development of Intelligence* (Flavell 1963).

ity to relate two variables to each other rather than to oneself develops at the same time as the ability to understand how two people relate to each other irrespective of oneself. The child who is ready to understand that mother is not also father's mother is likely to understand the relation of weight to volume in keeping the boat afloat. This sense of relativity contrasts with the earlier stage, when the child's world is ruled by absolutes. We are familiar with Jean Piaget's demonstration that the rules are *attached* to the game in the mind of the child at that early stage. This is not a peculiar, culture-bound phenomenon, for if the children in Piaget's Switzerland believe that the rules were made by William Tell or the Founding Fathers, then American children of the same age believe that the rules were made by George Washington or the pilgrims.*

Once a sense of relativity is achieved, the child will become more flexible in her adaptation. The following story illustrates the change from dependency on absolutes to the acquisition of such flexibility. At age seven-and-a-half, my daughter, Ellen, who was in a class with nine-year-olds, explained why she did not like to play soccer with the other children during recess: "It's like this. I like to play soccer at gym because the teacher makes us play by the rules. At recess the kids don't play by the rules." The point here is not merely what is known since the appearance of Piaget's classic work (1948)—namely, that at that age rules are seen as absolutes—but that at that age the child is *not able to engage in the required interaction unless the rules are presented as absolutes*. Ellen was not able to relate to other children under conditions of relativity of rules because she had not yet acquired the intellectual flexibility necessary for such an accomplishment. One does not need to put

---

*At least this was the opinion of my daughter, Ellen, when she was eight. The object here is not to pinpoint exactly the age at which each stage develops. For a good summary of the development of these stages, as well as further elaboration, see Kohlberg and Gilligan (1972: 182): "All movement is forward in sequence and does not skip steps. Children may move through these stages at varying speeds, of course, and may be found half in and half out of a particular stage. An individual may stop at any given stage at any age, but if he continues to move, he must move in accord with these steps. . . . No adult in Stage 4 has gone through Stage 6, but all Stage 6 adults have gone at least through 4."

oneself in the position of everyone else in the game, as Mead describes it, if one plays by absolute rules rather than by flexible rules; in the latter case, one must be able to relate the rules to the people who are engaged in interaction among themselves. It took Ellen another year, by which time she had reversed her liking for the game in the two situations. She said that she "hated gym" because "the teacher wants us to play soccer by the rules but [with considerable pride] *we* make *our own* rules."

The conception of the flexibility of rules—that is, the understanding that rules can be changed because they are rooted in the relationships among people—takes place at about the time when children begin to understand that their father is not also their mother's father. At this stage the child is able to understand how all others in the game relate to one another, and this is accompanied by a sense of power, as Ellen's pride in making "our own rules" illustrates. The understanding of some basic principles of mathematics follows the same process. Here my son Steven took his turn at age eight. He came home from school with an abacus, exclaiming enthusiastically that "this is the best toy I've ever had," and he proceeded to demonstrate multiplication with three figures. "Now let me test you," he said. "You do it." Pointing to successive rows of beads, I said: "It seems that first I must remember that these are the tens, and these the hundreds, and these the thousands . . . ." Here I was interrupted. "Wrong already," he said. "These beads are nothing, they have no value of their own." Then, lifting his head proudly and with a glimmer in his eyes: "They only have the value that *I* give them."

The discovery of relativity is an important landmark in the development of individualism. In Freudian terms, it is accompanied by an aggrandizement of the ego as children become aware that they can make their "own" rules or that beads "only have the value that *I* give them." This is how children discover their own power little by little, and one is reminded of the happy chuckle of the baby who discovers its power in picking up the rattle and throwing it on the floor repeatedly and having it returned; or, a little later, in the ability to hide an object and find it again. Growing up consists of successive discoveries of how things that have seemed *just to happen* can actually be brought about deliberately, changed and manipulated by one's own power. In this way, the understanding of relations outside the self helps develop in the young child the self-awareness that can be, as it is in modern society, the harbinger of adult individualism.

At the same time that children learn to differentiate between the game and its rules and between the particular role of mother and the person, they also learn to differentiate between motivation and behavior. Once they are able to understand that the rules are to serve the intended purposes of the players and therefore can be changed through agreement, they also learn that an act is to be judged according to the intention of the actor. At an earlier age, to repeat one of Piaget's classic stories, Johnnie, who in helping mother with the dishes drops a tray and breaks twelve cups, is judged to be "naughtier" than Jimmie, who breaks one cup when he tries to steal a cookie. Here the act is judged good or bad according to its external consequences. The act is part of the person. And the person is what the immediate consequences of behavior indicate.

It is only later, at the age of eight or nine at the earliest, that children learn to distinguish behavior according to the intention of the actor and learn that behavior is judged to be relative. The time at which this moral judgment develops is also about the time when the relativity of rules and the use of perspective in drawing objects have been learned.

Actually, moral and cognitive development continues up to age sixteen or later, according to Kohlberg and Gilligan (1972). They distinguish between an earlier stage, which they call "concrete-operational" (and which they say takes place, on average, between ten and thirteen), and a more mature stage, called "formal-operational" (between thirteen and sixteen). They illustrate these stages (p. 154) with an example from the work of E. A. Peel (1967). Children were asked what they thought about the following event: "Only brave pilots are allowed to fly over high mountains. A fighter pilot flying over the Alps collided with an aerial cableway and cut a main cable, causing some cars to fall to the glacier below. Several people were killed." A child at the concrete-operational level responded: "I think that the pilot was not very good at flying. He would have been better off if he went on fighting." In contrast, a formal-operational child said: "He was either not informed of the mountain railway en route or he was flying too low; also his flying compass may have been affected by something before or after take-off, setting him off-course, and causing collision with the cable." This last answer shows a willingness to consider alternatives, to figure out various possibilities; it is a trait that can be called intellectual flexibility in that it makes judgment variable in accordance with the position of the actor and the circumstances surrounding the act.*

It is important to note that modern legal thought is in large part based on the same principle. An investigating team with the task of establishing the guilt or innocence of the pilot in the above story would go about it in the same way as the youngster who considered the various alternatives. Yet a large part of the lay public is likely to argue that the law is the law no matter what the circumstances. This more "primitive" type of legal approach certainly corresponds to the mental orientation and sense of justice of many people. Kohlberg and Gilligan (1972: 158–59) have empirical evidence to support the hypothesis that "almost 50 percent of American adults never achieve formal-operational thinking." (They also found in their research that in simpler cultures, such as in the Turkish villages where they did their research, "full formal operations never seem to be reached at all, though it is reached by urbanized educated Turks.")

The examples of children's reflections on the circumstances surrounding the plane crash show that operational thinking is related to moral judgment. The second child, who was ready for multivariate analysis, so to speak, was ready to suspend moral judgment until various possible circumstances could be considered. He put himself in the position of the pilot, reflecting on the various ways in which the accident could have happened.

*Carol Gilligan (1982) has argued that this distinction between stages of moral development does not apply to girls in the way it applies to boys. I am not persuaded by her argument. For a discussion of her work, see Kerber et al. (1986).

Social and Cultural Differences

The structure of thought and of moral judgment differ under different social conditions, not simply as a reflection of culture but as a result of interpersonal experience. The extent to which intentions are taken into consideration may be the result of material circumstance. If, in a poor family, a child accidentally breaks twelve cups, the parent will most likely be upset even though the accident happened while the child was trying to be helpful. In contrast, if middle-class Johnnie takes a clock apart, his mother may be able to afford to be flexible in her judgment about his "scientific mind," a privilege of which lower-class Johnnie will be deprived if he has just put to pieces the only clock in the house.

However, material circumstances are not necessarily the main source of differential judgmental behavior. Following Piaget and Kohlberg, as well as some supporting empirical evidence to be presented later in this book, intellectual flexibility and complex mental operations seem to be related in some important way to the complexity of social relations. For example, people in the small peasant villages in southern Italy described by Carlo Levi in *Christ Stopped at Eboli* (1947) have a much harder time adapting to the differentiated society of the United States than immigrants from urban areas, where complex role relationships were gradually learned in the process of growing up. The strong solidarity and inward direction of *paisani* immigrant families in the United States at the beginning of the century helped them survive in the face of the unknown. Nevertheless, not having had any experience with the segmentation of lives imposed by American society and culture, such families found it hard to fashion social roles that would propel them into the mainstream. It was difficult, for example, for these rural immigrants to understand that at least some norms governing school life were unrelated to norms governing family life, as when a mother blamed a teacher for not teaching her son to listen to his mother (Covello 1967: 315).

In contrast, the mental differentiation essential in such a society was more easily accomplished by East European Jews who had experienced role articulation in the old country. They had dealt extensively with the distinctive realms of home, work, and religious institutions, as well as with officials and other members of the oppressive society. As Kramer and Leventman (1961) have argued, the assimilation of Jews in America was facilitated by their capacity to segment out various activities and relationships from their Jewish identity. Let us note here only that, if there is any basis in fact to Shalom Aleichem's stories and to the many jokes about Jews meeting on trains (cf. Freud 1960), then many Jewish men traveled from village to village and town to town in order to earn their livelihood, thus encountering strangers— officials, clients, peers—whose different ways had to be discerned and manipulated.

Role segmentation is especially prevalent in modern urban society. It became pronounced with the beginning of factory labor, when work became separated from the home. Weber (1947a) has shown that modern capitalism owes much of its rapid and forceful development to the separation of the workplace from the home. But industrialization generally, not only in capitalism, has profited from this separation. It made possible the exclusion of personal needs and desires, of affective attractions and distractions, from the rational pursuit of the efficient enterprise. The separation between activity systems did not affect all sectors of society at once. Primarily in rural society, but to a lesser degree in urban areas as well, many people continued to play their roles without much distinction of time and place. Even after factories became prevalent, many households still engaged in gainful work at home.

The sweatshop in the home of the small entrepreneur is an example of relatively undifferentiated labor. The prevalence of gainful work at home is another example. At the beginning of this century, immigrants to the United States, especially women, worked at home as part of their family duties, as when they took in boarders or engaged in sewing or flower-making in order to make ends meet. Nor was such work limited to one member of the family. Others in the household, including children, participated; the youngster who was sent by mother to deliver the finished goods to the employer and collect the pay may have also been told to use the proceeds to buy food on the way home.

Women, whatever their ethnic origin, considered their work at home as part of their task of feeding the family, not as a separate activity and certainly not one that conflicted with family obligations. Along with being wives and mothers, women at that time were economic managers *qui s'ignorent*.

To be sure, conflicts could arise in this undifferentiated way of life over what to do first—that is, over allocating one's time. These conflicts can arise in any system, and there are usually normative priorities to deal with them. The peasant woman, the immigrant woman, and the modern urban woman for that matter, will take care of her sick child first; the father too will probably pay more attention to his child when sick than he usually does when the child is well; family resources will be allocated to take care of such an emergency. Indeed, the term "emergency" indicates that tending to the issue has normative priority.

In every society there is a division of labor, however rudimentary, usually according to sex and age, in the routine of everyday living. But in premodern society, activities related to productivity did not necessarily take priority. When tending the baby, cooking, milking the cow, and preparing to go to the market were equally important, much energy that could be spent to produce was spent for family maintenance. Yet people must hardly have experienced a sense of conflict of allegiance.

Implications of the Modern Division of Labor

When work for production became separated from work for family consumption and maintenance, allegiances became divided. At work there was temporal and spatial isolation from personal worries and concerns. This introduced rationality into the activity system that would now be defined distinctly as *work*. It also introduced a split in the lives of workers, who, as Marx (1967: 292) so cogently put it, were "not at home when at work, and not at work when at home."

The realization that productivity is less likely to be interfered with when work takes place away from home is equivalent to the sociological observation that segmentation into well-defined activity systems is less likely to create disturbance in any of them. With the separation between the personal realm and that of work, new priorities evolved, and these were also more clearly defined.

This is not the place to recapitulate the fate of the working class in the early days of industrialization, when whole families were uprooted and women, men, and children were at work all their waking hours. It could hardly be said that there was a separation between work and home, since there was not much home life to speak of, if we believe Engels's (1926) description of the plight of the working class. For those early factory workers it would be more apt to say that there was spatial separation between working time and sleeping time. But with the development of industries, as some sort of order was introduced into the system (largely through successful class conflict) and as a more ordered family life became possible at the low rungs of the social ladder, a marked normative differential developed in the use of time and space between work and home.

As a consequence, today no two people share the same social space at all times of the day or week, and no one person is familiar with all the social spaces the other person occupies during the day. A person's place of work may be unfamiliar to spouse and children, and activities in voluntary associations may be individualized for each member of the family. Even persons who relate intimately to one another are not visible to one another in many of their activities. Moreover, we are unfamiliar with a large part of the world whose impingement we nonetheless feel strongly. Few of us know how frozen food or canned food is produced, or how factories, businesses, or churches really work. (This fact, of course, is bread and butter for sociologists and journalists, whose job it is to describe to the public the activity systems that remain more or less insulated.)

Paradoxically, even as modern individuals find themselves increasingly unfamiliar with their own societies, the horizons have widened. While we know less and less about how things work in our world, more and more of the world is visible to all—from the undersea world of Jacques Cousteau to riots in Manila, Seoul, and Israel. Yet as hospitals and courts and even intimate lives are projected on the screen, people continue to live and work in discrete realms, so that much of what touches our lives is little understood.

Peter Berger, Brigitte Berger, and Hansfried Kellner (1973: 78) speak of the "plurality of life worlds" in which individuals learn to differentiate as well as to synchronize their relationships, with a repertoire of alternatives that people have learned to reflect upon, through what these authors call multirelational synchronization. People make constant attempts to understand the unfamiliar and to locate themselves within it. This explains at least in part the success of the mass media. It may be objected that the mass media distort to some extent the reality that people want to comprehend, but this is precisely the point I am making: the distortion is meant to make the unfamiliar look familiar by appealing to characteristics shared by the public at large, characteristics that must remain on a superficial level if only because the larger the number of people being addressed, the less they have in common (Simmel 1950: 89–98). The media touch upon people's lives as well as on their fantasies born of limited experience. On the screen, life experiences as well as fantasized experiences "confront the individual with an everchanging kaleidoscope of social experiences and meanings" (Berger et al. 1973: 78).

While the kaleidoscope progressively enlarges in both size and complexity, its intricacies may be perceived but poorly understood. This fact has given rise to the notion that modern individuals are alienated, that they are strangers to the world they inhabit. Comprehension of this world does not come naturally to the modern individual, who has to search out meaning by articulating his or her relationships with others. Yet the fragments of a kaleidoscope can be discerned, even as they are changing. The colored bits of glass are triangles or composite triangles—squares and lozenges—not an undifferentiated mass. Experiences and meanings take place in a social structure that can be discerned, at least in its rough parameters. For the purposes of this book, these experiences and meanings will be limited to the social roles people play in their various status positions—that is, as they relate to others in differentiated settings. This strategy should make it possible to integrate the notion of multirelational synchronization into a set of verifiable propositions that can serve as the basis for systematic theorizing.

What appears on the phenomenological level as multirelational synchronization is seen from the structural perspective as role segmentation. If the kaleidoscope is seen as an agglomeration of social roles with the multiple and varied relationships they imply, it is possible to transform a confused picture into some conceptual order. The notion of role segmentation will help accomplish this transformation.

Implications of Role Segmentation

Role segmentation means that the same individual has different social roles that usually do not overlap. The spatial separateness of different activity systems—that of work, of family, and of voluntary associations, for example—helps maintain their social separateness. The important point about role segmentation is that in their various status positions people have different role partners, with each set of role partners remaining more or less distinct from the others. When moving from one status to another, a person must make mental adjustments to the new role partners.

The expectations a person brings to different relationships may be incompatible or even mutually exclusive. For example, an employer may expect an employee to be at work at a time when the employee must stay home with a sick child or attend to other important family matters. In such cases, the employee must articulate his or her role by asking, "Shall I stay home or go to work? Shall I behave as a family member or as an employee?"

The point is not only that conceptually the analyst can see some order in the ever changing kaleidoscope, but also that the interacting individuals themselves establish some order by articulating both how they are expected to relate to their various role partners and how they will do so. Faced with incompatible expectations on the part of various role partners, individuals have to decide how to fit in, even if the decision turns out to be unwise, even if they are bumbling and confused in the process. As Berger et al. (1973: 78–79) make clear, modern society "forces the individual into reflection," pertaining "not only to the outside world but also to the subjectivity of the individual." Hence, "modern identity is peculiarly individuated."

Individuation, the awareness of who one is in relation to others, takes place under conditions of role segmentation. I argue that the multiplicity of expectations faced by the modern individual, incompatible or contradictory as they may be, or rather precisely because they are incompatible, makes role articulation possible in a more self-conscious manner than if there were no such multiplicity. Although the multiplicity and incompatibility of expectations may constitute a psychological burden, they also provide an opportunity in that they foster self-conscious role articulation. Such opportunity varies, of course, with the extent to which social circumstances provide the possibility of making choices and of making them consciously and rationally. This is not to say that people who have such an opportunity always make conscious and rational choices, but that they are more likely to do so than they would in the absence of multiple expectations.

Not only do individuals play multiple social roles that are distinct from one another, but each role also entails different types of relationships. In the role of schoolteacher, a person relates to other schoolteachers, to the principal and to students, and even to some people with whom interaction is less frequent, such as the students' parents or the superintendent of schools. All these people, whether or not they have occasion to meet, constitute the teacher's *role-set*: they each have expectations of that teacher. By role-set I mean, along with Robert Merton, the complement of the role relationships a person has by virtue of occupying a particular social status. To cite one of Merton's examples (1968d: 422): "The single status of medical student entails not only the role of student in relation to teachers, but also an array of other roles relating the occupants of that status to other students, nurses, physicians, social workers, medical technicians" and, one should add, patients. The term *role-set* refers to all the role partners who relate to one status-occupant, the medical student in Merton's example. This differs from *status-set*, which refers to a person's multiple statuses and their associated roles with respect to all the relationships the person has. For the medical student, not only the role partners in medical school but also those pertaining to her role as daughter and perhaps wife and mother constitute her status-set.

This is because in each status position a person has a different role-set, and these sets may conflict in their demands for allegiance, as when the family claims priority from the professional woman and yet her professional associates expect not to be disturbed by her family obligations. In addition, the expectations emanating from role partners within each role-set can also be incompatible. The same woman, if she is a teacher, may face different demands from the principal and the children's parents; as a mother, she may have to take into account the expectations of neighbors as well as those of her children's teachers. The effort needed to conform depends in large part on the number of the partners she interacts with and on whether those partners do or do not share similar expectations. What Berger et al. (1973) have called in general terms the plurality of life worlds can be operationalized with concepts of role-set and status-set. This nomenclature makes it possible to bring conceptual order into a vague—though elegant—description and to account for the variability in the social behavior of the modern individual by specifying how individuals both differentiate and synchronize their relations with others and the relationships of others among themselves. It will help explain what Goffman (1961) has called the multiplicity of selves—which I will call role segmentation—through which individuals are able to alter behavior according to the situational context and with a repertoire of alternatives that has been learned through multirelational synchronization.

In contrast to the view that the plurality of social relations in modern society is a source of alienation (Berger et al. 1973: chap. 8), I shall argue that plurality of social roles is a source of role articulation and hence of individual enrichment. I agree with Sam Sieber (1974: 576) that "Role accumulation may enrich the personality and enhance one's self-conception. Tolerance of discrepant viewpoints, exposure to many sources of information, flexibility in adjusting to the demands of diverse role partners . . . all of these benefits may accrue to the person who enjoys wide and varied contacts with his fellow men" and, one should add, women as well. Plurality of social roles is synonymous with role segmentation, and it is the relative lack of opportunity for role segmentation that produces alienation in large sectors of the population within an otherwise segmented social structure.

The notion of segmented as opposed to nonsegmented roles suggests an important distinction between *simple* and *complex* role-sets. The distinction I propose is between a role-set in which most role partners do not differ much among themselves in status—one in which the role partners rarely change and are thoroughly familiar with one another, as in a family (as the root of *familiar* implies), and one in which, in contrast, at least several role partners are differently located in the social structure and are subject to change. It is not possible, of course, to specify at this time how many are "several." But the fact that we cannot say how many marbles make a pile should not stop us from identifying a pile of marbles when we see one.

The problem of contradictory expectations emanating from the diverse role partners exists mainly in complex role-sets. Simple role-sets are more or less homogeneous as far as the partners' social positions are concerned, and expectations of a status-holder's behavior are also more or less compatible. In those simple role-sets in which there is status heterogeneity, there is normative homogeneity in that mutual expectations are shared and are predictable because they occur among role partners who are familiar and whose demands are not subject to much change. When Merton (1968d: 424) speaks of the potential incompatibilities of expectations emanating from different points in the structure as a "basic source of disturbance," he must have in mind primarily modern middle-class society in which people usually operate within complex role-sets. It is under such structural conditions that the mechanisms Merton specifies operate to help diminish the disorderly effects of contradictory expectations.

The mechanisms for role articulation that I will summarize below also operate for status articulation—that is, for dealing with contradictory or incompatible expectations emanating from several role-sets. In this book I will speak of role-set and role articulation in the broader sense, referring to role partners in one as well as simultaneously in two or more role-sets, except in an exceptional case, as in Chapter 6. In that chapter I show that, in regard to the roles of women, role-set and status-set articulation have different social consequences.

Mechanisms for Role Articulation

The most important mechanisms, it seems to me, are those that refer to the distribution of power and to the fact of differential observability between role partners as well as to the structured interest in one another's behavior. That is, the mechanisms derive from the circumstance that role partners have different degrees of interest in the behavior of the status occupant—that is, they are not all equally involved with him or her—and that not all role partners are equally powerful in shaping a status-occupant's behavior, nor are they all equally in a position to observe his or her behavior. Moreover, "confronted with contradictory demands by the members of his role-set, each of whom assures that the legitimacy of his demand is beyond dispute, the occupant of a status can act to make these contradictions manifest. . . . This redirects the conflict so that it is one between the members of the role-set rather than, as was at first the case, between them and the occupant of the status" (Merton 1968d: 431).

This last mechanism calls attention to the fact that the individual status-occupant can make a deliberate effort to make it operate (Goode 1960). But this also applies to the other mechanisms. Insulation from observability, the limitation of the authority of power-holder, or his or her limited interest affords a status-occupant some measure of leeway for making decisions as to what expectations will have to be met. The professor who closes his or her office door for the day in order to write a paper, or a teacher who invokes a chairperson's announcement of a meeting against a student's request for an interview, are examples in point. The mechanisms of culturally established priorities (which will be dealt with in Chapter 6) can also be used, as when a physician is late at a staff meeting "because the patient comes first." Complex role-sets make it possible to use legitimate excuses or to claim legitimate commitments in selecting among one's multiple obligations or even to withdraw from some of them while one reflects about the differential nature of the commitments to several role partners variously located in the structure (cf. R. Coser 1975a). And to the extent that these mechanisms help individuals to articulate their roles, they also help to overcome the stresses and strains of different expectations.

In simple or restricted role-sets, the compatibility of expectations on the part of role partners usually makes it unnecessary for individuals to make these mechanisms operate and to reflect upon available choices. It must be noted, however, that contradictory expectations may face individuals in simple role-sets as well. In this case they often emanate from the same role partner, and this creates sociological ambivalence in the root sense of the term, as is the case with the merry-go-rounders and horseback riders described earlier. These instances illustrate the importance of the mechanisms of differential observability of a status-holder's behavior, for here this mechanism cannot operate. The merry-go-rounders and horseback riders were clowning because they were in full visibility of their peers. It is interesting to speculate what would have happened if some "thorough-going horsewomen" (Goffman) were present at the same time as the group of peers. This situation would be in one respect similar to that observed by many teachers when an embarrassed student carries out an assignment of giving a lecture to the class: the student is expected to be a student in relation to the teacher and an instructor in relation to classmates, by whom, moreover, he or she is ordinarily defined as a peer. And the teacher also wants the student to engage in the make-believe of being an instructor (cf. R. Coser 1979). The nature of the assignment would require a structure that precludes insulation from simultaneous observability by different role partners so as not to call forth embarrassment at best and inappropriate behavior at worst, as testified by the fact that in a classroom situation mentioned above students typically fail to perform to capacity.

In summary, a complex role-set is more likely than a simple one to offer mechanisms that help role articulation in the face of contradictory expectations, even if these are rare in simple role-sets. In addition to offering such mechanisms, complex role-sets offer more opportunity for individual initiative for making the mechanisms operate, thereby offering challenges for reflection, creativity, and role articulation. This point constitutes the main thrust of this book.

Thematic Content of This Book

The difference between a complex role-set and a simple (or restricted) role-set can be illustrated by the difference between the social role of the teacher in modern society and that of both a factory worker (Chapter 1) and a person embedded in a *gemeinschaft* (Chapter 4)—a structure in which relationships are stable and familiar and in which little effort has to be made to be understood and to understand others. As different as these two types of simple relationships are, they have one thing in common: they do not present the necessity, nor do they present much opportunity, for reflection about choices between available alternatives of behavior.

To the extent that an array of relationships with their different demands, expectations, and orientations requires from a person an effort to differentiate and to synthesize, a process of individuation exists. Modern society "forces the individual into reflection," pertaining "not only to the outside world but also to the subjectivity of the individual" (Berger et al. 1973: 78–79).

The proposition that, under social conditions offering predominantly simple role-sets, *the lack of a basic source of disturbance is also a lack of a basic source for reflection* is the thread that is being woven through this book. It will be examined in relation to the class and organizational structure (Part I), in relation to the social structure of gemeinschaft societies (Part II), and in relation to the position of women in modern American society (Part III).

In contrast to the view that sees role segmentation as a source of alienation, I shall argue that alienation is likely to occur where the conditions for individuation are absent. These conditions are not equally distributed through society. On the lower rungs, especially in organizations, people frequently operate on a level of simplified relationships—that is, under circumstances that provide only restricted role-sets. Such restriction, I shall argue, is alienating in that it does not offer individuals sufficient opportunities for exercising their judgment in regard to their own behavior and that of others. In Part I of this book I will try to show that alienation occurs in modern organizations mainly at the lower rungs of the hierarchy, where workers are not offered the opportunity of multiple and complex social relationships. Chapter 1 will examine some aspects of the alienation of factory workers. Chapters 2 and 3 will offer illustrations of some hospital structures where the role-sets of nurses are seriously restricted. These two chapters show that a restricted role-set fosters ritualistic or retreatist behavior. In addition, Chapter 3 illustrates that such behavior is associated with a weak self-image.

It should be clear by now that I believe it to be misleading to equate alienation with the absence of gemeinschaft. Persons who are enmeshed in a gemeinschaft may never become aware of the fact that their lives actually depend not just on what happens within the group but on forces far beyond their perception and hence beyond their control. A gemeinschaft may prevent individuals from articulating their roles in relation to the complexities of the outside world.

Part II will deal with the gemeinschaft type of social organization. In Mark Granovetter's (1973; 1974) conceptualization, ties in such a community are strong, yet opportunities as well as resources are restricted. I will try to show in Chapter 4 that such limitations also limit the development of abstract thought because the restriction of opportunities and resources, which derives in large part from the restriction in people's role-sets, keeps people in poverty; I believe with Virginia Woolf that, to the extent that this is so, "a poor child in England"—and she might have added in America as well—"has little more hope than had the son of an

Athenian slave to be emancipated into that intellectual freedom of which great writings are born" (1929: III–12).

In Chapter 5 I deal with some problems of family structure, showing the differential adaptation families make as a result of intrusion or nonintrusion into the family of the role segmentation in the society at large. Here I deal specifically with Granovetter's (1973) distinction between weak and strong ties in order to show that family structures that allow their members to have complex role-sets comprise weak ties in addition to strong ones and are therefore better adapted to modern society.

I attempt in Part III to apply the analytical scheme of role structure to an examination of the status of women in modern American society (Chapter 6) and return once more to the problem of embeddedness in a gemeinschaft (Chapter 7), this time as it affects the social roles of girls and women and some measure, however small, of cognitive orientation.

Part I

. . . .

ALIENATION

CHAPTER I

. . . .

Alienation of Labor

I n the imprecise terminology currently in use, the
term "alienation" refers to a generalized feeling of
frustration that comes over a person who is expected to behave in
a way that is experienced as not being "meaningful." In this view,
the several roles an individual has to play at different times and in
different places do not seem to express the true self, the true personality, or the development of an inner self. The source of this
diffuse uneasiness is often seen as the separation between different
activity systems. The unalienated individual is remembered, for
example, as one who was farmer and father and head of household and entrepreneur all at once. The nostalgic image is akin to
Toennies's notion of gemeinschaft—a concept modeled after rural
society—as opposed to *gesellschaft*, which is a term that denotes
"modern segmented structure."

The concept of alienation was given a more restricted meaning by Marx (1967). Counterposing the position and activities of
workers in modern manufacture and the lives of medieval artisans,
Marx did not apply the concept of alienation to modern life in
general but linked it to the condition of the working class. In
Marx's reasoning, the alienation of workers derives from the circumstance that they are deprived of the means of production, of
the product, and of knowledge about the process of production.

As a consequence they do not understand this process and do not derive satisfaction from the product of their labors. They do not have to interact much with one another for the accomplishment of their tasks, nor can they fulfill themselves in this important human activity. According to Marx, the condition of alienation is endemic in the division of labor, which is a means of exploitation.

This statement refers to role segmentation, as does Toennies's (1887) conceptualization of gesellschaft: a type of society where people relate to one another for specific ends, having hardly any other interests in common (T. Parsons 1949: 686–94). As the concept of alienation is used today, it frequently refers at least as often to the generally fractionated activities and relationships in modern society as to the more restricted relationships of workers with their employers, the product of their labor, and with one another.

Yet the positions and activities of industrial workers or of most of those who work in a narrowly defined hierarchy differ significantly from the segmented activities and relationships of individuals in many other social positions. Workers on the assembly line have a restricted role-set. On the job, operatives typically tend to relate to no more than one person in a position different from their own, the foreman. Other workers occupy the same position and have a similar status.

In other words, at the low level in the factory hierarchy, partners lack not only skills but also the social location of role diversity. In this operatives differ sharply from some white-collar workers and from professionals, who operate in a complex role-set: they relate to a variety of people differently situated in the social structure, and they therefore face different perspectives and expectations.* In the latter case, individuals must call upon a repertoire of behaviors and attitudes even though each single relationship requires the involvement of only a fraction of their dispositions.

I am reminded of the view expressed by Georg Simmel (1955)

---

*Diedrick Snoek (1966) uses the term "role-set diversity." He finds that role-set diversity is more common in supervisory than in nonsupervisory jobs. He also finds that role-set diversity correlates with tension. This, however, is not synonymous with alienation. I suppose that people in these positions often feel that, in their jobs, "there is never a dull moment."

who sees in such segmentation a structural basis for modern individualism. Not focusing on conditions of exploitation, but attuned instead to the way of life of the middle class, Simmel sees a person's participation in multiple activity systems as a source of individual freedom. In Simmel's view, the fact that an individual can live up to the varying expectations of several others in different places and at different times makes it possible to preserve an inner core, to withhold inner attitudes while conforming to various expectations. Moreover, in modern society a person partakes of several identities, some ascribed, others achieved. The particular combination of multiple identifications makes each person unique. For example, a person might be at once a Jew, an American, a sociologist, a Democrat, and a woman, and might have been born, let's say, in another country, worked for a while in the West, and now reside in the East—such a combination of attributes, each of which has left an imprint, is unique, since rarely would another person have the same combination of attributes.

Furthermore, the uniqueness of the individual is not solely due to the special combination of historical and demographic antecedents. In the present, the status positions I occupy, those of mother, teacher, writer, activist, friend—and the list could be extended to show that the gestalt is unique—gives me a distinct identity in relation to others. As Simmel (1955: 150–51) states:

> Today someone may belong, aside from his [or her] occupational position, to a scientific association, he may sit on a board of directors of a corporation, and occupy an honorific position in the city government. In this way, the objective structure of a society provides a framework within which an individual's . . . characteristics may develop and find expression, depending on the . . . possibilities which that structure allows. And the individual may add affiliations with new groups. . . . [The fact that he has that choice] gives him a stronger awareness of individuality in general, and . . . counteracts the tendency of taking his initial group's affiliations for granted.

Although Simmel's notion of the individualizing consequences of multiple relationships helps explain some important aspects of modern life, it does not come to grips with the concept of alienation as it was formulated by Marx, who saw it not merely as a state of consciousness but also as a property of the social structure. Igor Kon (1967) has called attention to the discrepancy between this notion and the use of the concept to denote an empirical psychological state, and so has Joachim Israel (1971). These authors point out that Melvin Seeman's (1959) distinctions between powerlessness, normlessness, isolation, and self-estrangement as different aspects of alienation refer to a state of consciousness.

Erik Allardt (1975) has shown that, of these properties, it is mainly isolation that refers at once to an objective and to a subjective state; that is, one in which the individual is interactively involved. He states that isolation is not only an emotional state and a form of behavior but also a property of the social structure in that it refers to conditions of exchange between individuals. But this can be said as well of powerlessness, normlessness, and self-estrangement, which indeed do refer to feelings and attitudes of aggregates of individuals as a result of social conditions, but which are also part of an interactional system in which resources are being exchanged asymmetrically. Allardt speaks of resources of power and resources of values, but I would like to speak more generally of resources inherent in the *social capital*, a concept that has been developed in some detail by Pierre Bourdieu (1980). The multiplicity and diversity of role partners—that is, a complex role-set—constitute such social capital.

I am referring here to the distinction I made in my Introduction between simple and complex role-sets. True, complex role-sets comprise multiple and differently located role partners and hence present individuals with various, often incompatible, or even contradictory expectations. But these are not only burdensome. They also constitute social resources for role articulation in that they impose the need for reflection about priorities and about compromises. Not everyone is in a social position that offers such challenges. Like most resources, complex role-sets are differentially distributed in the social structure, roughly according to social class. At the upper levels of the hierarchy, whether in the university, in government, or in industry—in the relations between management and staff—people are forced to negotiate and compromise with others of diverse interests, rank, and outlook and hence must take many factors into account, reflecting upon possible alternative courses of action. Melvin Kohn (1971) found that, contrary to the popular stereotype, bureaucrats (with education statistically controlled) "are found to . . . be more receptive to social change" and "intellectually more flexible" (p. 468) than nonbureaucrats.

A simple role-set such as one that exists in a narrow hierarchy offers only a limited number of choices of behavior. The social organization of the means of production and the distribution of power are such that factory workers on the assembly line can hardly avail themselves of mechanisms for role articulation. Michael Aiken and Jerald Hage (1966) found that rigid hierarchies and, related to this, a low degree of participation in decision-making account for alienation both from work and from what they call "expressive relations."

Alienation, in the sense used here, is more likely to occur in a simple type of structure than in a complex one, simple in the sense that the ties of solidarity formed are more likely to be the result of sameness than of interdependence.* This distinction between simple and complex role-sets is, of course, akin to Emile Durkheim's distinction between mechanical and organic solidarity, as Allardt (1975) also recognizes. But the stability and security achieved by mechanical solidarity may, under some structural circumstances, lead to a failure to recognize the imposed restriction of choices. In such cases isolation leads to powerlessness, which, however, may not be experienced as such. This happens in groups with strong outer boundaries, in which the relatedness of individuals in their total personalities to each other is so satisfying that isolation and powerlessness are obscured.

The fact that individuals are powerless does not mean that they experience powerlessness. To paraphrase Marx, there is powerlessness *in itself* and powerlessness *for itself*. Becoming aware

*There are, of course, many other sources of alienation—or should I say frustration?—in such manual jobs: repetitiveness, powerlessness, and lack of interest in or knowledge of the product. Some jobs are dangerous as well (see, among others, Halle 1984). Many of these features are related—some causally—to the fact of scarcity of social relations essential for doing the job.

of one's powerlessness is a first step in beginning to overcome at least some of it. Robert Blauner (1964) has shown how workers who are isolated in small groups hardly experience powerlessness, meaninglessness, and self-estrangement. He finds that "work in the textile industry, particularly because of its location in small Southern communities, fosters a narrow provincialism and lack of exposure to new stimuli and experience" (p. 87). "Workers are physically isolated and cut off from the larger society" (p. 88), but alienation is hardly felt. "Depending on one's perspective, the situation can be viewed as an almost idyllic folk society, or as a rather totalitarian community dominated by paternalistic management" (p. 88). This is akin to a gemeinschaft type of society and to communities of cults. I shall discuss this further in Chapter 4.

Although modern industry is in most respects considerably different from a gemeinschaft, it produces some effects that are similar. Where tasks are repetitive and seemingly unrelated to any end product, "work organization limits the employee to one segment of the product and a small scope of the process involved in its manufacture" (Blauner 1964: 172). As a consequence, not only do workers have a hard time understanding the process, but their isolation from other activities in the plant also limits their understanding of their own place in the process. "Textile operatives are confined to one room in the mill, which contains a department carrying out only one process of the dozen required for the completion of the product, and in that room they generally perform only one or two of the total number of productive tasks" (ibid.). Workers work next to one another but not with one another; their tasks do not depend on reflection, on choices between alternatives.

Blauner contrasts these conditions with those in the chemical industry, where work is automated. He finds that, under conditions of automation, workers can relate to one another in their work: "The perspective of the worker is shifted from his own individual tasks to a broader series of operations that include the work of other employees. The unique function of each operator is enmeshed in a network of interdependent relations with the functions of others. And responsibility as a job requirement demands thinking in terms of the collective whole rather than the individual part" (1964: 173).

Evidence supporting the assumption that complex role-sets are important for the formation of personal identity comes from hospital settings. One method used with mental patients in a therapeutic milieu is the psychodrama, which is, in effect, an attempt to create a mock role-set so to speak, for the person who experiences severe disturbances in interpersonal relations. By facing several role partners simultaneously on the stage, patients learn to perceive their roles in relation to these partners. Maxwell Jones (1953) describes a center where this method was used extensively for the treatment of "desocialized" patients who were "unable to hold jobs and prone to cause disturbances." In one case described by Jones (1953: viii), the actor was at first capable of performing only purely mechanical activities, such as drawing the curtains, which required him to face neither any role partner nor an audience. After repeated rehearsals he learned to interact with his role partners but still refused to face the audience. Later, he became capable of presenting himself to his partners and to the audience simultaneously.

It is worth considering whether the degree of complexity of role-sets for hospital patients offers an important distinction between a therapeutic and a nontherapeutic milieu. The theory advanced here seems to specify what many writers on the subject have called the nontherapeutic effects of a simplified social milieu. I have described how in a private mental hospital that was reputed for its therapy, the fact that each patient had two psychiatrists—one who controlled the relation of the patient to the milieu, the other who was the psychotherapist—each of whom had different expectations, made it possible for patients to rearticulate their lost identity (R. Coser 1979).*

The importance of role-set complexity for role articulation

---

*This is also illustrated by the account of Joanne Greenberg in *I Never Promised You a Rose Garden*. While the therapeutic skill of her therapist, Frieda Fromm-Reichman, is not to be underestimated, the sensitive reader can discern the effects of the patient's complex interactions with other patients as well as with two psychiatrists and other hospital staff.

also sheds light on an important problem in geriatrics: older people generally move in a more restricted role-set than younger people; if people having an impaired sense of identity are hospitalized, the further restriction of the number of role partners that hospitalization brings about accentuates their loss of identity. In many cases, it would seem, the deterioration of geriatric patients is social in the strictest sense of the word; it operates as a social process, no matter how hygienic, well equipped, and antiseptic the hospital, and no matter how well intentioned its personnel.

The mere existence of many departments and status groups in an organization does not in itself provide complex role-sets for its members. The complexity is determined by the number and type of transactions that must take place between members of the various departments and status groups. Although organizations may afford some members the opportunity for complex role-sets, different status-occupants have differential access to role partners variously located in the social structure. In large industrial organizations, for example, where complex role-sets may exist for some status-occupants, assembly-line workers, it will be remembered, usually have a restricted role-set since they have few role partners in social positions other than their own.

Some principles of bureaucratic organization, aimed at maximizing efficiency, rationality, and discipline by reducing the possibility of conflicting orders and expectations, may, when they are rigidly applied, have the dysfunctional consequence of so restricting the role-sets for some status-occupants as to alienate them from work and from colleagues as well (cf. Whyte 1951). It is worth investigating whether ritualistic behavior (for example, emphasis on rules) or retreatist behavior (such as "passing the buck") in bureaucratic structures (cf. Merton 1968c) is associated with a strong emphasis on going through channels, a procedure in which each status-occupant can approach only one or two other members of the organization and, conversely, can be approached by only one or two persons. Such a structurally built-in restriction on communication between members of an organization tends to isolate its members from the goals of the organization and encourage ritualistic behavior in their work. Narrow channels restrict the number of role partners differentially located in the structure with concomitantly different expectations of the status-occupant. This was illustrated in my case studies (R. Coser 1958) of two hospital wards, which I reanalyze in the following chapter.

· · · · · · · · · · · · · · · · · ·

CHAPTER 2

Innovation, Ritualism, and the Structure of the Role-Set

O bservations of medical and surgical wards in an urban hospital yielded some fruitful comparisons of different role-sets (R. Coser 1958). On the medical ward I observed in a New England teaching hospital, authority was consistently delegated down the line; only the intern gave orders to the nurse, and it was only with him that the nurse discussed patients. When interprofessional grievances turned up, nurses would take theirs up the ladder of the nurses' hierarchy, and the complaints would then come down the medical ladder until they reached the physician concerned. In this narrow hierarchy, nurses tended to be ritualistic in their behavior. In contrast, on the surgical ward, authority was not rigidly delegated. There, all physicians passed on orders to the nurse, and she herself took her problems to whomever they concerned; nobody objected if she dealt directly with other services in the hospital, such as the department of social work. As a result, nurses on the surgical ward showed initiative, worked their way around the rules when they considered it necessary, and saw themselves as important agents of the post-operative recovery of the patients.

The formal authority structure was essentially the same on both wards, with a simple organizational difference: on the surgical ward there was no separation of tasks among the interns and residents, who, under the authority of the chief resident, took care of any patient who needed their attention. On the medical ward, however, the chief resident delegated the care of patients to the interns, each of whom was in charge of specific patients under the chief resident's supervision. The interns passed on orders to the head nurse for the patients assigned to them. The assistant resident acted as supervisor and "consultant" to the interns.

The way in which the house doctors made use of the authority attached to their rank differed significantly on the two wards. On the medical ward, there was consistent delegation of authority down the line. The chief resident was heard saying on rounds to one or the other of the interns, "You make the final decision, he's your patient." The medical house officers also based their decisions to a large extent on consensus, with the chief resident presiding and leading the discussion. This differed from the surgical house doctors—interns and assistant residents—who received their orders from the chief resident; he was the one who made the decisions for the ward.

On the medical ward there was a scalar delegation of authority in a large area of decision-making, and the important decisions were usually made through consensus under the guidance of the visiting doctor or the chief resident. On the surgical ward there was little delegation of authority so far as decision-making was concerned, and decisions about operations and important aspects of treatment of patients were made by fiat by the chief resident.

Under these circumstances, surgical assistant residents and interns were more or less on the same level under the authority of the chief resident or the visiting doctor; this made for a common bond between assistant residents and interns and strengthened internal solidarity. Notwithstanding the formal rank differences among those who were practically excluded from the decision-making process, the relative absence of prestige-grading tended to eliminate some of the spirit of competition among the junior members. Moreover, with only little authority delegated to them, they could not be consistently superior in position to the head nurse. This "negative democratization," as Karl Mannheim (1951: 85) has called it, encouraged a collegial spirit between the nurses and physicians. Hence there was relative frequency of interaction and much banter and joking, which helped further to cancel out status differences (cf. Burns 1953; R. Coser 1960).

Since authority was scarcely delegated, all house officers passed on orders to the nurse, who in turn communicated with all of them. Writing orders was not the task of interns only. This was confirmed by one of the interns, who said: "Anyone on surgery writes in the order book"; the head nurse on one of the floors corroborated this situation when asked who gave her orders: "The interns, the residents also give orders, all give orders; we get orders all over the place and then you have to make your own compromise; you got to figure out what is most important."

These observations support the findings of Judith Blau and Richard Alba's empirical study (1982: 363) that "sheer complexity can undermine inequalities among bureaucratic units and occupational groups, and . . . organizational democracy is fostered when complex role relations promote extensive interunit communication." On the surgical ward, the relationship with the physicians put the nurse in a strategic position. In using her own judgment about the importance of orders, she made decisions about the care of patients, about delaying one action rather than another. It gave her a certain amount of power.

This position of the nurse on the surgical ward brings to mind Jules Henry's (1954) classic analysis of the social structure of a mental hospital. Henry discusses two types of social organization: the "pine-tree" type, in which authority is delegated downward step by step, as on the medical ward I observed; and the "oak-tree" type, in which orders come down to the same person through several channels, as on the surgical ward described here. The latter type, Henry says, is a source of stress and strain because the head nurse must follow orders coming from different directions that may or may not be compatible. This was probably true to some extent on the surgical ward, but it was accompanied by the increased power of the nurse and by her taking an active part in therapy.

Faced with the necessity of compromise, the head nurse on the surgical floor had to know a great deal about the conditions of patients; she had to contact them frequently and establish a fairly close relationship with them. This was all the more necessary since, during a large part of the day while surgery was being performed, most of the surgical staff was confined to the operating room. The nurse had to be "on her toes," checking with the intern on duty only if absolutely necessary, since he had his hands full. Her knowledge of the patients was greater than that of the nurses on the medical floor. A medical head nurse, although she tried to impress the observer with her own importance, admitted that "on surgical . . . the nurse knows more about patients than the doctor." The doctors, in turn, knowing that the nurse on the surgical floor had more contact with patients than they did themselves, relied on her for information and reminders, in this way increasing her influence and power of decision-making.

The physicians' expectations of the nurse differed according to ward. Asked to define a good nurse, the house staff on the surgical ward said that "she should have foresight and intelligence," or that "she must be a good assistant to the doctors," or that "she should read." Some even noted that the same criteria should apply to her as to a doctor. In contrast, the physicians on the medical ward emphasized the ability, in their words, to "carry out orders" and "do her routine work well." Only one of the medical interns declared that "intellectual curiosity is rare but nice if you see it," thus implying that he would not really expect it.

Where the rank hierarchy below the top decision-makers is not strict and the delegation of authority not well-defined, informal relations are built across status lines. House doctors on the surgical ward sometimes abdicated their authority if they could rely on the nurse. According to a surgical nurse, "The doctors want to be called in an emergency only, if they know you and they feel you know what you're doing. . . . They let us *do* things first and then call the doctor, as long as we would keep him informed." A third-year student nurse in the surgical ward had this to say: "In this hospital we're not allowed to draw blood or give IV's. I do it just to help [the doctors] if there are no medical students around."

Such informal arrangements clearly enhanced the nurse's prestige and enlarged her realm of power.

The surgical head nurse even made decisions about referral of patients to the social service. One of the head nurses, when asked whether she participated in social-service rounds, replied: "We should have been in on them, but I had close contact with the social worker, and I would ask her what I wanted to know. . . . Anyhow the patients would come to me for reference to the social worker." According to the formal rules, patients are referred to social service by the medical staff, but here, as in previous examples, the nurse by-passed official regulations and in this way maintained considerable control over patients.

Nurses on the surgical ward felt less tied to rules and regulations than nurses on the medical floor. This is illustrated by their reactions to the following story upon which they were asked to comment:

> *Interviewer*: I would like to tell you a story that happened in another hospital. An intern was called to the floor during the night to a patient who had a heart attack. He asked the nurse on the floor to get him a tank. She told him to ask an orderly. But there was no orderly around, and she still refused to get it for him. Do you think she had a right to refuse, or do you think he had the right to expect her to get it for him?

All nurses agreed that the nurse is not supposed to leave the floor if there is no other nurse around. However, while the answers of four of the five medical nurses were unqualified (e.g., "I would never have gotten the tank, the doctor definitely should have gotten it," or "I wouldn't think of leaving the floor for a minute when I'm alone, this is unheard of"), all five surgical nurses made important qualifications (e.g., "she should have called the supervisor," or "she could have said, you keep your ears and eyes open while I get it," or "she could say, if you keep an eye open in the meantime, I'll run and get it"). Surgical nurses were more accustomed than medical nurses to finding a way out, to using initiative, and to circumventing rules and regulations if necessary.

Nurses are often accused of being ritualistic, of attaching

more importance to routine and rules than to the ends they are designed to serve. Although nurses on the medical floor were accused fairly often by interns of "merely clinging to rules" and "not willing or not able to think," nurses on the surgical floor were never the targets of such criticisms. Indeed, surgical nurses seemed to be capable of innovation and were often relied upon by physicians to use their own judgment and to initiate action, as I have shown.*

In his classic paper "Social Structure and Anomie," Merton (1968c) traces ritualistic behavior to pressures emanating from the social structure, specifically to the malintegration between declared goals and the means available for implementing them. We can now specify what accounts for such malintegration in the case at hand. Nurses on the medical ward were deprived of the means for achieving the consensual goal of optimal care because the narrow line of command restricted the number and the diversity of role partners. A restricted role-set obviates the use of mechanisms for role articulation because these operate under conditions of complexity of role-set. The ritualism on the medical ward was a manifestation of alienation, which is, as I have suggested, endemic in a social structure that simplifies the role-set of its members. It will be remembered that in complex role-sets, where demands, expectations, and challenges emanate from different (structurally determined) perspectives, there are mechanisms available for dealing, at least in part, with the multiple and often contradictory demands of role partners who are differently situated in the social structure.

It seems to me that workers in the chemical industry, as described by Blauner (1964) and mentioned in Chapter 1, have a

---

* It might be objected that surgical nurses were better educated than the nurses on the medical ward. Indeed, the problem of pre-selection is hard to solve. In this hospital, the nurses were recruited from its own school of nursing. Still, the surgical nurses might have been brighter. Melvin Kohn has tackled this problem in his work with Carmi Schooler, with refined statistical techniques. They demonstrate that, with education controlled, effects of the occupational experience of job complexity are at least as strong as are the reciprocal effects of occupational self-selection and of job-molding processes, perhaps even twice as strong (Kohn and Schooler 1973).

more complex role-set than those in the textile and automobile industries. Automation seems to afford the opportunity if not the necessity for workers to relate to other employees in order to accomplish their tasks, and thus to broaden their vision and to articulate their roles in relation to the various people they must relate to. The process of activities in a complex role-set tends to set in motion the use of mechanisms for role articulation as it also did for the nurses on the surgical ward I described. Such a role-set (i.e., one that includes role partners who occupy different positions from one another) offers, at the same time that it may make incompatible demands, structural opportunities for role articulation that are inoperative in simple role-sets. Although the potential incompatibilities of expectations emanating from different positional points in the structure can be a source of disturbance, the very threat of disturbance presents a challenge for its prevention and thus encourages the members of the role-set to make use of mechanisms that help diminish the disorderly effects of contradictory expectations.

As I stated earlier, within the same structure mechanisms for role articulation are not equally available at all levels of the hierarchy. On the medical ward described above, it was the nurses—not the physicians—who suffered from a restricted role-set. Whether in a hospital or a university, in government or in industry, it is usually people at the upper levels in the hierarchy who have a complex role-set, which forces them to negotiate and compromise with role partners of diverse interests, rank, and outlook, taking many factors into account and reflecting upon various alternatives of action in relation to a variety of others.

The opportunity structure is such that there is an unequal distribution of available social mechanisms that permit or challenge people to articulate their roles. For factory workers at the assembly line, or for nurses on some hospital wards, there are hardly any such mechanisms because these workers are part of a narrow hierarchy where they relate to few people in the structure who are in positions different from their own. Hence, they are not challenged to articulate their roles in relation to others. It is not only that at the lower end of the hierarchy people have little power by definition; to this must be added the alienation that comes from restricted role-sets.

The next chapter will compare a context of structurally induced alienation with a complex structure, one that, similar to the findings in another of Judith Blau's (1980) studies, "engenders a high level of humane care and expert treatment" (p. 277).

CHAPTER 3

Anomie and
Restricted Role-Set

At Sunnydale Hospital on the West Coast, there were five buildings comprising 28 wards, with a total of 650 beds, which were all defined as serving the "terminally" ill, even though the wards ranged from active treatment (eight) to custodial wards (twelve).* Approximately 100 additional patients were lodged on six wards of another building; this was a rehabilitation center, here referred to as the Center. In Sunnydale proper, nurses had few relations with professionals other than a small number of fellow nurses. There was hardly ever a physician on the floor, let alone any other health personnel. Although several interns were assigned to the wards, there was a tacit understanding that they need not be present. An intern explained that he found the nurses "outstanding" because they were "ultraconservative in calling the doctor," and a nurse explained why she did not have conflicts with physicians: "I have nothing but pleasant experiences. They know I'm only trying to help them, keep them from coming over here."

In contrast, the Center had its own director and medical staff. Nurses worked with different professionals who also held differ-

---

*This chapter is a revision of an analysis first presented in R. Coser 1963, which also includes a complete tabular analysis and a description of the coding procedure.

ent status positions. Each nurse had to deal with four physicians. There was always at least one physician on the wards, and one day a week all four were present. On that day staff conferences were held mornings and afternoons. Nurses also interacted intensively with several occupational and physical therapists, two psychologists, and a psychiatrist. The nurses who had these diverse role partners cited instances of how different physicians prescribed different courses of treatment, or of how a physical therapist expected different scheduling for a patient than the physician's prescription had led the nurse to expect: "It puts the burden on me. I have to make the decision." The differences and incompatibilities between their various role partners gave the nurses at the Center a measure of autonomy. It turned out that they also had different images of themselves in relation to their work than did the nurses at Sunnydale proper. In all their responses in interviews, Sunnydale nurses were more likely to focus on routine activities or settings; Center nurses, in contrast, related their statements to patients or professional relationships, thus indicating the salience of social relationships for their work.

In answer to the question "How would you describe a ward at its best?," sixteen of the seventeen Sunnydale nurses, but only one of the ten Center nurses, referred to the physical appearance of the ward, indicating that routine housekeeping problems stood in the foreground of their attention. A typical Sunnydale description of "a ward at its best" was: "When it is finished and you stand at the head of the ward and look in, it is beautifully done, everything is clean." Center nurses, in contrast, referred to the behavior of patients, as in the following typical answer: "I like to see everybody out of bed and as active as possible. I like a certain amount of, not humor, but at least a cheerful, informal ward setting."

The emphasis by Sunnydale nurses on physical aspects in contrast to the emphasis on human achievement by Center nurses is consistent with their perceptions of their needs. Asked "What are the most important things needed in your ward?," only one of the seventeen Sunnydale nurses but five of the ten Center nurses mentioned improvements that would benefit patients or benefit relations among staff members or between staff and patients. The answers about "needed improvements" are also consistent with answers to questions about sources of satisfaction and dissatisfaction. Center nurses expressed professional concerns, usually emphasizing staff relations or achievements with patients, whereas Sunnydale nurses usually referred to the physical aspects of "the job." Sunnydale nurses focused on paperwork, the shortage of personnel, or other routine matters. In contrast to the *organic* conception of work at the Center, in which concern was focused on human implications, was the *ritualistic* concept of work found at Sunnydale, where the focus was on dead matter and work was mechanical. As one Sunnydale nurse cogently explained: "Well, my dear, I don't know. There isn't anything that I find unpleasant. *I have done it so long, I just automatically do it*" (emphasis added).

Sunnydale nurses were not deeply involved in their work. Although they did not dislike it much, they had no important reasons to like it much, either. Center nurses, however, seemed to have strong feelings about sources both of gratification and of frustration. Asked "What do you like least in your work?," most Sunnydale nurses mentioned some routine as a source of dissatisfaction, such as "I don't like removing impactions." Furthermore, their references to sources of dissatisfaction were not expressed with much feeling. The first impression upon interviewing Sunnydale nurses was that, if there were any dissatisfactions, they did not involve professional issues. The example given by the nursing director illustrates this point: "There are not a great many grievances. A year ago they had complaints about the parking situation; they had to park the cars too far from the buildings. So now we've changed that."

The complaints of Center nurses, however, showed concern with professional relations and professional issues. Eight out of ten Center nurses but not one of the seventeen Sunnydale nurses mentioned some aspect of professional relations or some conditions of patients as sources of dissatisfaction. One Center nurse stated, "The thing I like least is the stress I feel when we have such a tremendous working organization and we can't communicate to get the job done." Another said what she liked least was "when some patients get exasperated." In addition, these typical statements were expressed strongly, while Sunnydale nurses' responses were given in a flat tone of voice.

Sources of satisfaction also differed between the two groups. All Center nurses said they derived satisfaction from professional relations or professional achievements. One nurse, typical of the others, said that what she liked best was "taking someone who is crippled or injured and showing them the means so that they can be self-sufficient, and seeing them accomplish it. It's a tremendous challenge." The sources of gratification for Sunnydale nurses, in contrast, concerned professional achievement or professional relationships less frequently (seven out of seventeen). The responses were more likely to be in general than in concrete terms; the nurses liked, they said, "the care of humanity" or "nursing care." One Sunnydale nurse implied that her gratification stemmed from being able to get away from work: "It's a well-rounded day, . . . and the employees can put in requests for vacation." Sources of both dissatisfaction and satisfaction in relation to their work tended to be of little consequence to Sunnydale nurses.

Although in this small piece of research I was dealing with only one professional group and a small number of cases, my findings call into question the notion that alienation from work is synonymous with dissatisfaction. To be sure, alienation may be associated with a sense of boredom and with the feeling that the work does not make sense, but in at least some situations, such as the one at Sunnydale Hospital, these go together not with acute dissatisfaction but with indifference. Strong feelings of both satisfaction and dissatisfaction seemed to be associated with involvement in one's work, at least in this case.

The different attitudes toward work in the two settings were also revealed in the images nurses held of themselves in regard to their work. Center nurses seemed to have a stronger sense of professional identity. Everett Hughes (1971b: 339) has called attention to the importance of a person's work for an experience of self: "A man's work is one of the more important parts of his social identity, of his self; indeed, of his fate in the one life he has to live, for there is something almost as irrevocable about the choice of occupation as there is about choice of a mate." So much is this the case, Hughes suggests, that when you ask people what work they do, they are likely to answer in terms of "who they are"; that is, they attempt to establish and validate their identity by referring to their work in a publicly recognized and preferably esteemed occupational or professional category.

In the interviews with nurses reported here, it was the Center nurses who gave self-enhancing descriptions of "who they are" when asked "What is the most important thing you do?" Nine out of the ten Center nurses referred to their inclusive role; half of them used nouns rather than verbs to describe their tasks. From them we hear: "I am a team leader . . ."; "I think setting sort of an example . . ."; "Well, teaching. . . . This puts me in the kind of a position of a staff counselor"; "The RN is . . . a go-between the supervisor and the team . . . a diplomat, that's what it is, politician." These nurses conformed to Hughes's description of those whose work defines their social identity.

In contrast, only two of the seventeen Sunnydale nurses referred to their inclusive role. An additional two said they could not answer the question, and thirteen mentioned some specific task, like "carrying out doctors' orders," "seeing that the patients are fed and cared for," and "medicines and bedside care." These nurses took the question of what they did literally; they did not substitute for the verb ideas that would connote their identity. This would suggest that, when Hughes says work is one of the most important parts of a person's social identity, he refers to one type of work and one type of person: relatively unalienated work and relatively unalienated people. But in industrial society, many types of work and work situations do not lend themselves to the formation of a sense of identity. The prototype of such an alienated work situation is, it will be remembered, the assembly line. Alienation, in Marx's sense (1956: 169), means that "the work is external to the worker, that it is not part of his nature, that he consequently does not fulfill himself in his work but denies himself. . . . It is not the satisfaction of a need but only a *means* for satisfying other needs."

This seems to describe fairly well the meaning of work for Sunnydale nurses, which seems to be similar to that of the industrial workers studied by Robert Dubin (1956). He found that work was central to the lives of only 24 percent of the interviewed workers. This differs from the finding in Louis Orzack's (1959) study of registered nurses that, for 79 percent of these professional persons, work was indeed a central life interest. But at Sunnydale work did not contribute substantially to the nurses' sense of social identity. They mainly performed task-oriented routines. This raises the question of whether a routinized mechanical view of tasks and alienation of self in the work situation is associated with a different perception of the social field. Marx had something to say about the relation between fragmented labor, alienation of self, and estrangement from others: "[The worker] works next to others, but not with others. This is, in the last analysis, the alienation of man from man; individuals are isolated from and set against each other. . . . Man's alienation from himself is simultaneously an estrangement from his fellow men" (Marcuse 1941: 279).

How did the nurses in my research relate to their social milieu? It turned out that of the eleven nurses who expressed their identity by defining their role inclusively, nine described a "good-looking ward" in terms of the people who occupied it; but of the fourteen nurses who gave a restricted description of their work, thirteen saw the ward in terms of routine housekeeping tasks. (Two Sunnydale nurses who did not answer the question about the most important thing they did also defined a good-looking ward in terms of housekeeping.)

The connection between conception of work role and perception of the social field is highlighted in drawings the nurses were asked to make of "a nurse at work."* Eight nurses drew a picture of a nurse without a patient; one of these nurses was at the Center, the seven others were at Sunnydale. This graphic presentation of "the nurse at work" without a partner gains significance when it is compared with the nurses' conceptions of their "most important task." The drawings exhibit an association between the way nurses depicted themselves in relation to others and the "most important thing they do." Two of the nurses did not answer the latter ques-

---

*This method was suggested to me by Hans Mauksch in an oral communication.

tion, it will be remembered, but of the fourteen nurses whose answers suggested task-specific images of their work, eleven drew pictures of a nurse only—that is, without showing a patient or any associate—or they claimed that they could not portray the role at all, thus indicating that in both instances they did not see themselves as relating to patients. Of the eleven nurses with inclusive images of their roles, ten included a patient in their picture of "the nurse at work." They exemplified the thesis of G. H. Mead (1946: 164) that our selves exist and enter into our experience only so far as the selves of others exist and enter our experience.

The differences in the nurses' drawings add relevance to their differing reports on sources of work satisfaction. All the nurses who reported deriving satisfaction from professional achievement included a patient in their pictures, and so did the nurses who said they derived satisfaction from professional relations. But none of the nurses who spoke of satisfaction in terms of general care depicted the nurse as part of a social arrangement in their drawings. Relevant too are the nurses' notions of improvements needed in the ward. As will be remembered, six nurses, one from Sunnydale and five from the Center, focused on better staff relations or on better care of patients when describing needed improvements; all six included a patient in their drawings of "a nurse at work."

Alienation from work seems to be associated with alienation from other people, as well. The nurses who drew a picture of themselves only, when asked to draw a picture of "a nurse at work," expressed their social isolation—a distinctive attribute of alienation, as I have shown in Chapter 1.

Indeed, the isolation of Sunnydale nurses might be observed directly in relation to their interaction patterns. As can be expected, of all the observed interactions, staff-patient interactions were significantly more frequent at the Center than at Sunnydale. In two weeks of systematic observations, the following activities were noted: staff-patient interaction, staff occupied with patients without eliciting response (staff acting "on" patients), and staff-staff interaction. These were examined in relation to the types of wards that were the focus of this research.

In addition to the distinction between Sunnydale and the

TABLE I   *Type of Interaction as Percentage of All Observed Interactions*

Type of interaction	The Center	Active treatment	Sunnydale long-term treatment	Custodial	Total number of observed interactions
Staff acting on patient without eliciting response	11.2%	32.0%	30.4%	33.5%	105
Staff-patient interaction	57.5*	34.0	30.4	20.8	125
Staff-staff interaction	31.3	34.0	39.2	45.7	147
Total number of observed interactions	80	85	69	144	378
Total number of minutes observed per ward	72.5	54.0	71.3	81.7	
Number of wards	6	8	8	12	

SOURCE: R. Coser 1963.
    *This is a conservative figure. If interactions had been timed, the rate of staff-patient interaction at the Center would be even higher. At the Center, it was not unusual to see a nurse working with a patient for some time.

Center, a distinction within Sunnydale between its custodial, long-term, and active wards is revealing. In Sunnydale's custodial wards, many patients suffered from complete mental or physical deterioration, which makes either for complete helplessness or for other disturbances such as incontinence or inappropriate aggressive behavior. Since these wards suffered from an acute shortage of personnel, one would expect that staff would be very busy with patients. However, this was not the case. As Table 1 shows, on custodial wards staff members interacted with one another much more frequently than they acted on patients, even without eliciting response.

This finding is paradoxical indeed, but it can be explained if we realize that the staff interactions that were observed took place only between nurses or aides and not between different professionals. Because of the excessive demands that the helplessness and mental disturbance of the custodial patients impose on an exceedingly small staff, professional activity seems almost pointless. Rather than attempt to deal with patients, nurses as well as orderlies were often observed withdrawing from the ward and seeking support from one another in the nurses' office, over a cup of coffee or a cigarette. These interactions usually did not involve professional concerns. They should therefore not be confused with interprofessional relations centered on tasks at hand. For example, the observer noted such scenes as the following: "When I left the ward (at 3:55 P.M.) only one aide was still on the floor, reading a magazine in the linen room. I relayed a request by a patient for a bedpan. She thanked me, but five minutes later had not come out. Janitor joined her and they were chatting as I left." There is further evidence of withdrawal, as the head nurse of one of the custodial buildings testified: "We have so much absenteeism and tardiness. Today two people were supposed to be on duty, but they didn't show up. That is the most irksome quality here. . . . So many of them feel that the hospital work is the last work; if they have something to do downtown, that comes first."

Conditions in the custodial wards were extreme; so was the rate of staff-staff interaction. The latter seems, however, to illustrate a general trend. As a comparison of all types of wards confirms, the frequency of interaction among staff correlated with patient-nurse ratio (Figure 1), a seemingly unexpected result: the larger the patient load, the more staff tended to spend time among themselves.

Not only was there a tendency for ad hoc withdrawal from professional tasks at Sunnydale, but there were also mechanisms that fostered the systematic withdrawal of professional staff. Most staff activities that were observed were those of nurses and aides, in part because there were relatively few physicians. There was one full-time staff physician in charge of Sunnydale's 650 patients. He was assisted by four or five interns, who were sent out from the city hospital of Maplewood for a period of six to thirteen weeks. The interns rotated between the five buildings (with two or three wards each) and the emergency room, so that each was in charge of the same 100–150 patients for only two or three weeks. An intern explained how he handled this situation: "I try to let the nurses keep me up on everything and then I try to weed out those that can wait a couple of days; after they have been let go, in a fair majority of cases, it will clear up by itself. . . . The cases that are more interesting to me, I spend more time on and let the other

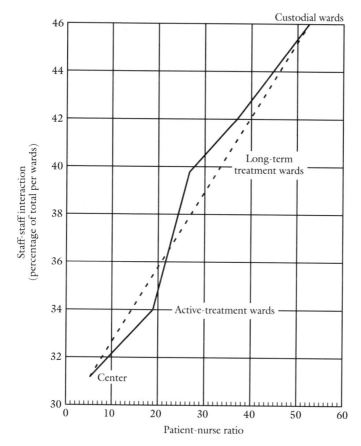

FIG. 1. Staff-staff interaction rate by patient-nurse ratio on a typical winter day (cf. Table 1). From R. Coser 1963.

ones go." Faced with more patients than they could possibly care for during their two-week stay in charge of a building (in some cases an intern is in charge of two buildings), interns do not even feel called upon to be active and they cease to feel harassed. As several conversations with interns made clear, they looked forward to their Sunnydale assignment because they expected it to be an opportunity for rest ("This is the only time in my training that I can afford to go to the library," one of them explained).

An acute shortage of personnel does not necessarily increase each person's load; if it gets bad enough, understaffing legitimizes withdrawal from the task. A nursing supervisor illustrated this point: "The intern would go through the charts on his day and never change the prescriptions; sometimes he would just add to the old prescriptions, and *we* can't change them." The fact that Sunnydale interns as well as nurses engaged in retreatist behavior derived from the circumstances that, first, only a few professionals actually encountered each other, and, second, mechanisms were at work that would make for the mutual avoidance of the few professionals on the premises.

Therefore, the paradox of the almost linear correlation between the rate of staff-staff interaction and patient-nurse ratio can be resolved if seen within the structural context of professional life at Sunnydale. There were not many professional groups, the main ones being those of nurses and interns. There was a social service, but social workers stayed in their offices, since they dealt almost exclusively with the administration; their main task concerned the eligibility of patients for admission and the collection of old-age pension and insurance. The following comment by the nurses' supervisor who reported that interns do not change prescriptions illustrates how interprofessional relationships could be a source of social control: "When the new staff physician came *we told him*, and he went over all the prescriptions and took the old ones off the list" (emphasis added). Such social control by nurses over physicians (or vice versa) was relatively rare at Sunnydale because of the lack of diversity in social roles; in this case, control had to wait for a change at the top of the medical hierarchy.

Not only did interns withdraw from the wards, but, more important still, nurses and interns also helped one another to maintain this type of withdrawal. Physicians did not interfere in the active-treatment ward when the buzzers at patients' bedsides were disconnected and the electric cord tied up so that patients could not use the bell. An employee in the administration building commented on this practice: "The patients can't reach the bell to call the nurse; they can't reach the water. . . . When the nurse walks out the patient can't call for help." In turn, nurses knew, as one of them said, that if they "call a doctor without too much need he doesn't like it," and consequently they were, in the praiseful words of one intern, "outstanding since they are ultra-conservative in calling the doctor." Another intern thought that the nurses were not always reliable since, as he explained, "they sometimes call for minor things." A nurse's competence was apparently measured not by her achievements but by her willingness to help the physician ignore the patients. Where sanctions were at work at Sunnydale, they often pressed for the evasion of norms. It is partly on this basis that some consensus between physicians and nurses was established. "They know that I won't ask them to come unless I need them"; these words of a nurse point to such consensus.

Consequently, Sunnydale was characterized by a lack of those interprofessional conflicts that usually occur in other hospitals. But lack of conflict is not necessarily functional for an organization. As in this case, it may be a result of relative withdrawal from the task (cf. L. Coser 1956: 83–85). One nurse in an active-treatment ward explained that she had little difficulty with physicians: "I have very little contact with interns. They go their own way." Not only were there too few physicians to be "underfoot"—a frequent accusation in other hospitals—and not only did they stay too short a time for strong sentiments—either positive or negative—to develop, but the interaction between nurses and physicians was further curbed by the encouragement of mutual avoidance by both professional groups. Lack of conflict only thinly disguised latent hostilities. One nurse who said she "never had any trouble getting along with doctors" went on to say: "I feel sorry for an intern who thinks he knows it all before he leaves. He's in for a rude awakening." Hostility was expressed this way by another nurse who said she experiences "no difficulties" with doctors: "The nicest thing is that they don't stay with us forever."

For readers of George Homans's (1951: 334–68) analysis of Hilltown—a New England town in which the normative system had become weak—Sunnydale may touch a familiar chord. As in Hilltown, at Sunnydale *the number of activities that members of the group carry on together was small*. As in Hilltown, this does not mean that individuals had nothing to do. Like the Hilltowners who had little to do *with* other Hilltowners, in Sunnydale nurses had little to do *with* other professionals. As a consequence, *the low frequency of interaction was associated with weakness of interpersonal sentiments.* The indifference noted in regard to satisfaction and dissatisfaction with work, as well as the reported lack of difficulties with doctors, speaks to this point. Low frequency of interaction and weakness of interpersonal sentiment have a mutually reinforcing effect so that sentiments are not strong enough to motivate the members of professional groups to collaborate with one another.

The structural determinants of alienation can be highlighted by their opposite at the Center. The staff there was characterized by its multiple professional affiliations, and mechanisms evolved that ensured a large measure of social control. The various professional groups worked alongside one another, in collaboration with one another, and often in competition with one another. The staff included ten physicians (one a psychiatrist) in part-time capacity, several physical and occupational therapists, two psychologists, two social workers, and twelve registered nurses, supplemented by practical nurses who took an active part in treatment. There was also a part-time speech therapist, and there were occasional visits from outside social workers who represented a foundation or a community vocational service.

As we have known since Durkheim, the interdependence of various occupations resulting from the division of labor brings about the "organic solidarity" that helps hold modern society together. This solidarity is between interdependent status-occupants who are involved with one another. They are bound by common interests, though they may be in conflict over the means of implementing them. In some settings, such as the Center, they can observe one another at close quarters, where they are all under pressure to orient themselves to differential expectations in these complex, criss-crossing circles. Persons of various status positions and different professional orientations and expectations are bound together by their common commitment to the concrete goal of returning patients to the community; there is strong concern on everyone's part with achievement and failure. And precisely because of this zeal, conflicts arise. Indeed, all nurses at the Center reported difficulties with physicians, whereas only five of the seventeen Sunnydale nurses did so. As one Center nurse explained: "Everybody feels that they like to be in charge of the situation. Everybody says, 'This is my business.'"

The greater frequency with which Center nurses reported difficulties with physicians was not merely the result of difficult relationships between diverse professional groups in a complex work setting. The contrasting reports of Center and Sunnydale nurses also reflected the fact that, at the Center, conflicts were freely described to the interviewer because they were being articulated and carried out openly on the wards. Fighting over controversial issues was considered legitimate. Differences of opinion and expectations were voiced at regular and frequent staff meetings, and this provided a patterned opportunity for dealing with conflicts between the different professional groups and for articulating issues and everybody's relation to these issues. At the meetings, the goals to be pursued and the norms that should govern behavior were continuously invoked (cf. L. Coser 1956: esp. chap. 6).

The following exchange at an all-staff conference is an example of the usual but not always friendly discussion of issues:

> *Physician (addressing physical therapist)*: How come this patient hasn't been going on with her program?
> *Physical therapist*: She says she doesn't like it.
> *Physician*: Is that a reason for stopping it?
> *Psychologist*: Doctor, you forget that this patient knows that she has less than five years to live.
> *Physician*: If you see it that way, we may as well have a concentration camp instead of a hospital.
> *Psychologist*: But don't you see that there is a reality situation here?
> *Physician*: What's the reality? That we all have to die?

Here we have an articulation of the dilemma facing health care at the same time that the staff is being reminded of the medical norm that, so long as there is life, efforts have to be made at prolonging it. But in this controversy the physician is also being reminded that the goal of rehabilitation should be applied with flexibility.

Indeed, in both types of wards the definition of the goal determined treatment of all patients. At Sunnydale, all patients were defined as terminal whether or not they were. As a consequence, at the same time that it made the staff feel powerless, this definition was responsible for the poor allocation of professional resources. This restriction of the professional role-set exacerbated the staff's feeling of powerlessness at the same time that it left the definition unchallenged. This is a good example of how powerlessness and isolation on the job is a property of the social structure.

It must be noted that, at the Center, the definition of rehabilitation was also indiscriminately applied; all patients were considered treatable whether or not they were. But there, in contrast to Sunnydale, thanks to the complexity of the role-set, the definition could be challenged, as in the above example. In this complex situation, normative control was exercised at all levels of the hierarchy.

In the following example, a physician is the object of normative control:

> *Psychologist to physician-in-chief*: May I remind you, Doctor, before this patient comes in, that he is very anxious, and that much of his response at this conference will depend on how he is being talked to.
> *Nurse*: I would like to add that this morning the patient was very upset about . . . (*description follows of upsetting situation*).
> (*Patient is brought in, interviewed, and led out again.*)
> *Physician-in-chief to psychologist*: How did I do, teacher?
> *Psychologist*: Go to the head of the class.
> *Physician-in-chief* (*addressing the conference of about thirty people*): In this place, if I look over one shoulder, there stands a psychologist; if I look over the other shoulder, there stands a sociologist. (*Smiling*) This is some way of practicing medicine! *

The staff meeting provided an occasion for exchanges between professionals of various types and statuses. In this way conflicts were brought to the level of rational discourse and instrumental

---

* This was said in a jocular tone because this physician, who was the director of the Center—the late Leon Lewis, to whom I am indebted for his generosity in supporting my research—was himself responsible for the condition he laughingly criticized. He repeatedly stressed, privately and publicly, that the best way to practice medicine is within an interdisciplinary framework and that staff meetings and conferences are essential for good medical practice.

behavior. The exchange of opinions and judgments gave a professional definition to personal involvement. It provided ways of dealing with conflict situations at the same time that it elicited individual efforts from all.*

Social control was reinforced by the fact that the meetings provided institutionalized settings for *observability* between persons of various fields of specialization and in various positions in the hierarchy. I need not belabor the point that, if persons variously located in the social structure are to evaluate the behavior of others, they must at regular intervals see one another behave or at least be in a position to obtain information about one another's behavior. If such information is lacking, occupants of a particular status become exempt from the judgment of competent colleagues, and role performances may sink below tolerable standards (Merton 1968d: 376). At the same time, the meetings largely limited the time and place of observability, thus ensuring a patterned measure of insulation—a mechanism, it will be remembered, available in complex role-sets.

The conferences and meetings at the Center did more than provide information about the professional behavior of those in the social system. They also made status-occupants aware of the differing expectations held by role partners significant to them. The following incident shows how a nurse facing differing expectations was forced to think about her obligations: "Miss R. has battled with Dr. B. and some of the others because they all said they knew what the nurses' responsibilities were. He wants the nurse to carry out procedures that, according to Miss R., are physical therapy procedures. True, it's a mistake to make jacks-of-all-trades of us." She continued thinking about the role of the nurse: "This doesn't mean that we don't have to know what the other person does. In a rehabilitation service where there are no physical therapists, it's surprising what the nursing service can accomplish." Another nurse reacted to conflicting expectations in this fashion: "We have been taught by Dr. X. that this patient must always catheterize himself. On the unit another doctor said

---

*Cf. L. Coser's (1956: 48–55) distinction between realistic and nonrealistic conflict.

we have to get away from these catheterizations. I have two days
to clear up the matter." In the process of coping with contradictions derived from such significant role partners, the nurse was
likely to form an image of herself as a significant actor in the social
system. It is not surprising, then, that this nurse, when asked to
describe the most important thing she does, said it would be
"along the lines of a tremendous teaching service and continuity
of responsibilities . . . that go over and beyond the patient-care
aspects."

A property of social structure like that of the Center, which
facilitates articulation of the nurses' roles, was the presence of a
sufficiently large number of registered nurses in one unit. Every
nurse knew that she was not alone in facing contradictory expectations of many role partners. The nurses could therefore articulate
their roles collectively, as in the following incident. Several nurses
reported complaints coming from patients about the "doctors'
manners" in violating privacy: "Doctors and other staff charged
into their cubicles when they had their curtains drawn without
knocking or warning or anything, or maybe knock and walk in at
the same time." Another nurse: "The patients know that they have
a right to their integrity and their privacy." She added: "The patients have a right to expect *me* to do something about the problem they bring to me because this is *my job*." Yet, as everyone who
is acquainted with hospital etiquette knows, a nurse cannot call a
physician to task. In most hospitals, she will have to go through
channels; a complaint about a physician will in all likelihood go
through the intermediary of the nurses' director and the chief of
service. But at the Center a nurse did not find it useful to appeal to
the nurses' director, since, being associated with Sunnydale proper,
she was considered an "outsider" by Center personnel. Center
nurses, bound to the Center staff by common norms and patterns
of professional exchange, were more loyal to Center physicians
than to Sunnydale nurses of whatever rank, and they used their
initiative in dealing with physicians. How this could be done was
explained by the nurse whom we heard describe physicians as
"charging into the patients' cubicles"; the privacy problem, as well
as others such as "one doctor telling one thing and another doctor

telling another one," led her to call a meeting: "I said, why don't we have a meeting with the doctors? . . . We, that is, the registered nurses, all went. . . . We told them, and of course then their annoyances came up too, but they were very accepting."

The fact that all nurses shared similar difficulties and that there were avenues for verbalizing them made it possible for these issues to be removed from the level of personal problems to that of social organization. The nurses were in a position to discuss personal problems in terms of their professional roles. Thus, the nurse who called the meeting said that "teaching" was her most important task, and added, "This puts me in the position of a staff counselor." At another point in the interview she implied the ways in which relations between nurses helped to articulate roles: "I have to go to informal staff conferences every morning and ask for their report, and this again is nice too because the supervisor and the head nurse can *use me as a sounding board* just as well as can the staff" (emphasis added).

At the Center, then, the conditions and mechanisms that provided a source of social control—multiplicity of role partners, conflicts between professional groups, mutual but limited observability, and regular meetings to deal with conflicts—also provided the conditions for the articulation of roles and formation of professional self-images.

These conditions did not prevail at Sunnydale. The goal of caring for terminally ill patients, as it was understood at Sunnydale, restricted the staff's task primarily to problems of housekeeping. Status-occupants suffered from restricted role-sets—that is, from a restricted number of significant role partners. This had the following consequences: First, Sunnydale nurses (as well as other status-occupants at Sunnydale) worked under conditions of *low observability*—a condition that resulted in the reduction of social control. Second, since there were few persons *differentially* located in the social structure, there were hardly any conflicting expectations facing the status-occupants; the latter were, therefore, not required to be *continuously engaged in articulating their roles in relation to the members of their role-sets* and, consequently, in forming a professional self-image. Third, given their scarcity, registered nurses were deprived of role partners of similar status, so that there was little opportunity for them to articulate collectively, as professionals, the limitations and responsibilities pertaining to the relationships they shared. Sunnydale nurses were isolated both from peers and from other professionals.

We recognize here the absence of mechanisms that would have helped alleviate the burden of contradictory expectations. In other words, where a few contradictions exist, there exist no mechanisms that can be called into play, and this deprives individuals from any leverage for the articulation of their roles.

The fact that a restricted role-set prevents workers from relating to their work in an unalienated and individualized fashion has also been noted by William F. Whyte (1951: 306–7). He observed that "long, narrow hierarchies . . . are relatively low in economic efficiency and in employees' morale" and that in such organizations people are prevented from "discovering what their strengths and weaknesses are" and from "feeling that they themselves have really mastered their jobs."

With mastery comes a secure self-image and also a mind-set that allows intellectual flexibility. Kohn (1971, 1978) finds that "substantive complexity of the job" is specifically pertinent for explaining flexibility in dealing with ideational problems. Although "job complexity" is not exactly the same as "complexity of role-set," there is good reason to believe that the two notions are fairly similar.*

As I have also shown, where individuals are more likely to be confronted with incompatible expectations, they are required to reflect upon an appropriate course of action in relation to their status position. They must decide whether to abide strictly by the rules or to reinterpret or even defy them, and they must weigh each decision in relation to their own purposes of action and the purposes of others. This calls for innovation, sometimes in the

---

*In Kohn's (1978) analysis, substantive complexity is an overall measure, based on a factor analysis of information obtained about complexity of work with data, complexity of work with things, and complexity of work with people. The correlation between the substantive complexity of the job as a whole and the complexity of work with people is .82.

form of violation of custom and hierarchical modes, as when the surgical nurses described in Chapter 2 were giving intravenous injections in violation of hospital rules, or when Center nurses repeatedly stated that "here we have to teach the doctors." It also forces a certain measure of flexibility, as differences are ironed out through negotiation and compromise, through a social process that forces each participant to take into account the vantage point of the other person.

To these traits must be added another important ingredient of this type of interaction, namely empathy. Merton (1968d: 436) shows that this psychological trait is fostered by arrangements in a social structure in which people face conflicting expectations:

> The extent to which empathy obtains among members of a society is in part a function of the underlying social structure. For those who are in the role-sets of the individual subjected to conflicting status-obligations are in turn occupants of multiple statuses, formerly or presently, actually or potentially, [and therefore] subject to similar stress. This structural circumstance at least facilitates the development of empathy.

Indeed, Alex Inkeles (1984: 15) found that the capacity for empathy distinguishes the modern person, who lives in a complex society, from the traditional person. This raises an important question: if reflection, flexibility, and empathy have roots in the social structure, at least in part, we must ask whether there is a relation between social structure and mental abilities. It implies that not only behavior but also the thinking process itself would seem to be related to the nature of social relationships. This will be dealt with in the next chapter.

Part II

GEMEINSCHAFT

CHAPTER 4

. . . .

The Greedy Nature of Gemeinschaft

F rom what has been said so far, it should be clear that social environments differ in the extent to which they provide the kind of relationships that challenge individuals to reflect about expectations facing them, as well as about their own roles in their interactions.* In groups that offer complete security, in which role partners hardly change, and in which mutual expectations remain stable, there is relatively little opportunity to innovate or to weigh alternatives of thought and behavior. A gemeinschaft is such a group. Its members know one another and are oriented toward one another cognitively and emotionally. They count on one another, expecting to receive and give support. This differs from understanding one another, which, following Weber's definition (1947a: 55–57), means that they are consciously sensitive to one another's motivations and experiences. In a gemeinschaft, people are likely to take one another for granted. Each knows what the other is all about without having to reflect on it. Relationships are generally satisfying, so one does not look much for outside sources of gratification or to outside resources for achieving specific ends. When the immediate environment—say, members of one's family—is found wanting, there are others,

* An earlier version of this chapter is to be found in Powell and Robbins, eds. (1984: 221–39).

71

neighbors and friends, available close by to be addressed and relied upon.

This ideal-typical if not idyllic image of gemeinschaft does not exclude hostilities, fights of any sort, or violence in particular. As anthropologists know only too well, even family relations—in spite of, or rather because of being close—can be governed by mutual suspicion. Feelings generally, love and hate, are on people's sleeves, as they say. Homicide rates and other types of aggression may be as high in gemeinschaft as in gesellschaft societies, or even higher.* Fights are personal regardless of whether or not people team up with one another to give vent to their sense of justice. Brutality, like love and generosity, is given easy expression.

In this type of society, boundaries between family and the surrounding community are not rigid. Families provide for their members strong links with the community so that these two institutions are both indispensable and meaningful to each other. What happens to the members of the community and to its institutions is important to every family and is being sanctioned by all. Individuals are integral parts of both of these mutual support systems, in which one gives oneself as one expects to be given to.

To be sure, in simple societies that approach Toennies's type, people also play several roles, but these are all part of the person and are undifferentiated by time and place. The British anthropologist Max Gluckman (1962: 27) describes this situation:

> A man plays most of his roles, as several kinds of productive
> workers, as consumer, as teacher and pupil, as worshipper, in
> close association with the people whom he calls father and son
> and brother, wife and sister; and he shares citizenship with
> them, that mediated citizenship which is so marked a feature of
> tribal constitutional law. Moreover, all these roles are played on
> the same comparatively small stage, of the village and its en-
> virons, where shrines are placed about the huts or in the cattle
> corral, where the baby is born and the dead are buried, where
> the year's provender is stored.†

* Henry and Short (1954) have demonstrated that homicide rates and suicide rates are inversely related, with homicide generally being more frequent in stronger relational systems, and suicide more frequent in weaker ones.

† The modern building boom both in suburban residence and in urban office space, while stemming from many economic and social sources and

Similarly, in the gemeinschaft that Toennies had in mind, people led relatively undifferentiated lives in which social, moral, economic, and religious activities were integrated. Their commitments to one another usually had priority over other commitments.

Greedy Institutions

I believe that a gemeinschaft has something in common with a type of social organization that Lewis Coser (1974) has called "greedy institutions," referring to institutions that demand total commitment from their members. He describes and analyzes some social mechanisms by which total commitment can be obtained: celibacy, as in the case of the clergy in the Catholic church; or its opposite, promiscuity, as in the free-love movement of the early Communist Party, or as in some Utopian communities like Oneida (see also Kanter 1968); eunuchism, as in the Byzantine Empire; or extreme differences in social origin that prevent crisscrossing relationships between the greedy institution and the original reference group, as in the case of court Jews or some courtesans of the French court. These cases, as different as they are in their manifest patterns both historically and sociologically, share one structural feature: the fact that individuals are cut off from current or prior cathected relationships on the outside and thus are made dependent on the institution that claims their moral allegiance and the totality of their efforts.

Greedy institutions have something to offer those who have outside contacts or who sacrifice their prior or outside relationships: for example, upward mobility, as in the case of court Jews or courtesans; freedom from slavery, as in the case of eunuchs; a common cause, as in some political movements or utopias; and, in all cases, an enhancement of ego as a consequence of a sense of being needed. These institutions also offer a new sense of belonging to those who feel isolated, deprived, or uprooted.

Most cults also are greedy institutions, and they appeal to a

serving a variety of purposes, can be seen also as serving to maximize spatial extension in a society that grows in complexity.

large number of people. It is estimated that there were some three million members of cults in the United States in the 1980's. What I call the "Jonestown syndrome" is that of a group of individuals who have been led to forfeit their ties with the outside and who become self-destructive because of their self-sufficient interdependency. Extreme as this case may be, it is the gemeinschaft feature of the commune that attracted followers, that made them cling to their lives in common as they were led to their deaths (Coser and Coser 1979).

Jonestown was extraordinary in its "greediness" to the point of claiming its members' lives unto a common death. It is mentioned here to illustrate a point: that communality, strong allegiances, and so-called meaningfulness, important as they may be, are not enough to ensure either a viable society or individual development. To be sure, not all greedy institutions are as greedy as Jonestown. They come in different intensities of greediness. But utopias and similar communities have in common an insistence on complete devotion and on as complete a break as possible with the outside and with the past.

Integrating Lewis Coser's conceptualization with Merton's role-set theory, we can now identify one structural property of greedy institutions: they operate under conditions of restricted (or simple) role-sets. This is what appeals to many who yearn for a sense of belonging, and it is what helps to give the gemeinschaft character to such communities. The greediness consists in claims for priority in the allocation of material and emotional resources. The gemeinschaft is greedy to the extent that it absorbs individuals in unidimensional relationships, depriving them of the opportunity to confront multiple and contradictory expectations that would make them reflect about their roles. And in a gemeinschaft, role-sets are restricted.

Where roles-sets are simple, role partners generally share the same role-sets and are of well-defined status. In Lewis Coser's example of the traditional parish, the priest in the Catholic church deals mainly with the church hierarchy and the church members. Since he is assigned to a village other than his own, under premodern conditions of transportation his personal interests are not so likely to interfere with the interests he has in his parishioners by virtue of his position in the clergy. While he may have conflicts with the mayor of the town, as in the village of Clochemerle in Gabriel Chevallier's famous novel (1963), it is to be noted that this conflict is intense and pervades all other relationships. There is no other conflict in the village that distracts from this main conflict and that would distribute antagonisms and alliances.

The Restricted Nature of Gemeinschaft and Its Adaptation to Modernity

This type of social organization is ill-adapted to modern society. The rural village or town can no longer be experienced as a unified way of life inside some boundaries beyond which one cannot *see*. While the impact on people's most personal lives comes from unknown sources sometimes long distances away, the external boundaries between groups have become fluid if they have not disappeared altogether. The farmer's town or family in the Midwest is linked to the vagaries of Wall Street, and the fate of the Detroit worker is linked to Japanese technology. Whether or not to get married at a certain time, what education to give one's children, whether or not to seek early retirement—such personal decisions that are based on one's income depend on the world market more than on gemeinschaft norms.

Within gemeinschaft groups in modern society, the strong ties that bind people together, although useful for the lubrication of the system by providing cohesion and reassurance, are insufficient by themselves. The Midwest farmer or the Detroit worker, like any individual, needs to be informed about events and organizations that exist beyond the boundary of the immediate group, and the various members of the group need to have networks outside, preferably different ones, because such networks serve as resources for survival.

The following is a dramatic example of strong gemeinschaft ties. The Dutch paper *Het Nieuwsblad* (April 1, 1979) reported from Rawalpindi: "Twelve members of one Pakistan family were asphyxiated in a well last Monday. This family drama took place in a village a hundred kilometers west of Rawalpindi. The first victim had gone down into the well in order to fix a broken pump. When he did not come up again, number two went to look. He didn't come back either. This went on until the twelfth family member had gone down into the well. Then a fellow villager hit on the idea that the motor might be exuding toxic gases. He alerted the police" (my translation).

This story contrasts with one printed that same year in the *New York Times* (December 15, 1979), according to which an eight-year-old boy in Illinois responded to his four-year-old brother's fall into a 40-foot well by throwing two life preservers into the well, calling the telephone operator for help, and then running for assistance.

These extraordinary incidents dramatize the difference between people who are embedded in a gemeinschaft and those who, in Toennies's terms, live in a gesellschaft type of society, in which the institutions of the society are both differentiated and intertwined. The members of the Rawalpindi family had little concept of their relatedness to the outside world; they merely related to one another. Such a family could be called extremely centripetal—a notion I shall come back to later. I only want to mention here that partners in centripetal relationships turn back upon each other and depend on one another for problem-solving. The role-sets of these individuals are clearly restricted within the context of a small group, which is the sole focus of their attention.

In spite of the fact that conformity can be better ensured where expectations can be more easily met (P. Blau 1977: 96–98), closely knit groups, even though they give individuals a feeling of security and a sense of belonging, have less survival value, at least in the modern world, than those that permit or encourage their members actively to pursue relations with individuals or groups on the outside and to orient themselves toward other institutions for their needs. This is because such rigid conformity does not permit readaptation to changing circumstances and conflicting demands, which is what the modern world is all about.

This does not mean that primary relationships within modern society are harmful to individuals or subgroups. On the contrary, they are needed for fostering the bonds of solidarity within the body social. This is what Charles Horton Cooley had in mind when he talked about the social importance of *primary* groups (Angell 1956: 23–31)—that is, groups stemming from fate, like the family or peer group, in which individuals participate with their whole personality and in which they are embedded through face-to-face interaction.

Kingsley Davis (1949: 289–309) has contrasted this type of structure with *secondary*—that is, instrumental—relationships. In these, roles are segmented, entered into deliberately for one or more specific purposes. In such groupings individuals give part of themselves in one place for a specified time and another part of themselves in some other place, again for a specified time. To the objection that time spent in the family or with friends is in many instances limited and specified and that participation in primary groups is segmented as well, the answer has been that empirical reality usually differs from the ideal-typical distinction.

While this is correct, it begs the question. Nor do I mean to emphasize the familiar fact that in empirical reality people do not live up to ideal expectations. We deal here with something more fundamental in that the segmentation stems from the differentiation of institutions, and it is for this reason that it intrudes upon gemeinschaft relationships. Where the production of goods and the learning of skills take place in different activity systems than the family, this encroaches upon the family's activities and obligations at least some of the time.

If instrumental activity systems were not permitted to intrude—that is, if primary groups were to remain the predominant type of structure—then these would offer poor tools of adaptation to modern life. In themselves primary groups tend to be restrictive both of opportunities and of the thinking process of individuals, in addition to being ineffective in dealing with crises. They tend to isolate individuals and groups from the recognition and hence the manipulation of universalistic events and relationships.

The Nature of Particularistic Relationships

The distinction that Talcott Parsons (1951: 61–63) made between particularism and universalism serves us well here. A simple or restricted role-set is usually one that is particularistic—that is, where the parties are, as the word indicates, particular to each other, unique and irreplaceable. Such are relationships between siblings, between husband and wife, and between friends. Not that a person cannot have more than one sibling or several friends. But each of these relationships is unique in that it provides a different kind of satisfaction or dissatisfaction, as the case may be. Gemeinschaft relationships are mainly particularistic.

Not all simple role-sets are particularistic. For example, as I have argued in Chapter 1, assembly-line workers have simple role-sets because they deal with other workers who have similar status positions and with only one who has a different status, the foreman. The relationships among the workers are universalistic in the sense that in their working roles they can be replaced. So, too, are the relationships between buyer and seller, patient and physician, employer and employee.

These two types of relationships are not strictly dichotomous. Not only are there some rare occasions when my friend might give me a job, but more to the point is the fact that frequency of interaction (Homans 1951) also helps introduce some particularism into universalistic relationships so that even a relationship between a buyer and a seller, if repetitive, may contain particularistic elements. It does not have to come to the point where the bachelor marries his housekeeper or a female psychiatrist her male patient. Sentiments and loyalties develop that have an influence on the job, as episodes like the Watergate scandal, the Iran-Contra affair, and other forms of corruption amply testify.

Particularistic sentiments are not necessarily dysfunctional for universalistic relationships. They may provide bonds that strengthen a sense of mutual obligation and facilitate friendly negotiations. In other words, particularistic feelings lubricate the system in that they satisfy and protect the individuals concerned. They help overcome the rigidities of universalistic relations. It is easier to work or to exchange goods or services with someone one likes as a unique individual; it is easier to communicate, to exchange ideas.

There is a tendency to invest sentiments in one's relationships so that universalistic relationships are more likely to change into particularistic ones than the other way around. Particularism is a greedy force (as cronyism readily illustrates). It could operate as a sort of Gresham's law, driving out universalism, which therefore has to be shored up against its pull.

Where particularistic relationships predominate, the outside world is not the primary focus of attention, and particularistic relationships become ends in themselves; that is, they tend to be greedy. This greediness manifests itself in a tendency to restrict the actors' role-sets as we have seen. Unless there are, in Granovetter's term (1982), "bridges" that tie the primary group members to other groups and individuals—bridges that serve as reminders of extrinsic purpose—then particularistic relationships have a weak potential for attaining goals, overcoming crises, or finding new adaptations where necessary. Such bridges are likely to be provided by role partners who have different positions in the role-set.

Who helps whom and how become important questions in the analysis of group integration. Relatives and friends, those with whom we have particularistic ties, help us in our daily needs—such as when we need a little financial aid to tide us over, when our health gives out, or when we have a flat tire on the road in the middle of the night. Those with whom we have universalistic relationships give us jobs, help us carry out our responsibilities, meet and consult with us when we have to achieve specific ends, enter into commerce, or provide connections for further achievement.

Bernard Farber (1971: 13–14), in commenting on Claude Lévi-Strauss's (1949) theory of marital selection as a form of reciprocal alliance between different kin groups, calls attention to the fact that there are two types of reciprocity (mainly, I would like to add, at the two extremes of the stratification ladder): one consists of exchange, the other of mutual support. The first is more prevalent among the well-to-do, for example, as a basis of marital selection. Material resources get pooled and, since they are not needed for immediate consumption, get enhanced. In contrast, the type of reciprocity that consists primarily of mutual support is more characteristic of relationships among the poor. Here also resources get pooled, but these are resources of a personal nature or of a minimal material nature, for immediate consumption, that can hardly be used for extrinsic purposes. (Between these two extremes the two types of reciprocity can be mixed.) The latter type is described by Carol Stack (1974) in her study of a poor community. Food or money is borrowed, returned as soon as possible, or reciprocated as necessary.

Stack also shows that, among the poor, networks of reciprocal support are more likely to consist of kin, whereas in the middle class they consist largely of acquaintances (cf. Granovetter 1982). Insofar as acquaintances tend to be of differing status and from different regions, they constitute a complex role-set and provide more varied resources. It is important to note here that mutual support, if provided by kin or close friends, takes place in a restricted role-set and helps maintain the static conditions of the poor by increasing their interdependence and hence some measure of greediness in the relational system. That is, the very fact of near-exclusive closeness of relationships contributes to the lack of mobility.

This, then, is another sense in which gemeinschaft is greedy. It holds on to its members in a simple role-set of mutual support that is centripetal, and it prevents the opening up of avenues for opportunities at the same time that it prevents the development of individualism. J. V. Ford, D. Young, and S. Box (1967: 372) had restricted role-sets in mind when they wrote: "Friends emerge from the undifferentiated category of individuals of similar status. . . . Hence, interpersonal approach behaviors will be concerned with demonstrations of willingness to share; this may be in swapping, lending, or even passing the ball in a game. . . . As the demands for reciprocity intensify, both the number of friends it is possible to have and the frequency of extra-friend interaction will be restricted." This may lead "to a lack of differentiation between friends and self and a minimization of unique behaviors."

In particularistic relationships, "expectations of performance . . . are phrased in terms of who a person is instead of what he has accomplished" (Cohen 1971: 25). People remain tied to concrete individuals. They know each others' problems—explanations and apologies are not as necessary as they would be with mere acquaintances—and they remain focused on their concrete problems as well. This raises the question of the effect of universalistic and particularistic relationships on the manner of communication and reflection about self and the world around us.

Communication and Cognition

In restricted role-sets, the partners are satisfied with a restricted vocabulary. This is so because close relationships do not require much verbal elaboration. We have all experienced those gratifying moments when words are not needed or when one word suffices to convey a world of meanings. Among intimates, meanings do not have to be spelled out or clarified. But such language is not useful for communicating with outsiders, those who do not share the close relationship.

L. S. Vygotsky (1962: 148) notes that, between people in close psychological contact, words acquire special meanings understood only by the initiated. He calls this "inner speech," speech in which a single word can be "so saturated with sense that many words would be required to explain it" to the less initiated. It often sounds like a private language; for example, sentences do not have to be finished: "When the thoughts of the speakers are the same, the role of speech is reduced to a minimum" (p. 141). He quotes Leo Tolstoy in *Anna Karenina*: "Now Levin was used to expressing his thought fully without troubling to put it into exact words: He knew that his wife, in such moments filled with love, as this one, would understand what he wanted to say from a mere hint, and she did" (Vygotsky 1962: 117).

In contrast to such restricted speech among people who are close, speech in which people do not depend on intimacy and may not even know one another has to be more elaborate. As Basil Bernstein (1971: 175–76) states: "Universalistic meanings are those in which principles and operations are made linguistically explicit. . . . Meanings are less tied to a given context . . . they are in principle available to all because the principles and operations have been made explicit." Hence, we can distinguish with Bernstein between *restricted* and *elaborate* speech. The first is simpler and is typically used in particularistic relationships. It is more dependent on others, whereas elaborate speech can be understood by everybody. Particularistic meanings are "more context-bound, that is, tied to a local relationship and to a local social structure" (ibid.). When participants are engaged only in particularistic relationships, they become dependent on one another, and their language becomes restricted to the common taken-for-granted meanings. The nature of their relationships affects the thinking process. If only a word or two is needed to convey "a world of meanings" in a daily routine, then not only does the language become impoverished, but the meanings do not become conceptualized and cannot be used as readily to influence or help modify the behavior of others, as interactions or conversations are supposed to do.

Particularistic relationships have a parallel in the particularistic notions people have of inanimate objects. We can easily agree that a lemon and an orange are different fruits, each being particular. But in order to articulate in what sense they are similar, we must abstract from some of their properties and go through the following thought process: although the colors are different, the tastes are different, and the sizes and shapes are different, oranges and lemons are equivalent in one respect: they both have vitamin C. To claim that a number of fruits are called citrus fruits and have this quality in common is to find something *universal* about them.

Michael Maccoby and Nancy Modiano (1966) compared Mexican children from a *mestizo* village with children from Mexico City and from Boston on what they call equivalence tests. The children were shown several objects and asked to point out the differences among them as well as their common features. It turned out that identifying differences was not a difficult task for any of the children. But on the identification of equivalence, "by about age nine . . . more than twice as many urban as rural children succeeded at [these] tasks. By [age] twelve, the difference [between the children] has become fourfold" (p. 263).*

Similar results were obtained in Senegal and among the Eski-

*The success on the equivalence task proved to be unrelated to school achievement or to the language-free Raven's Progressive Matrices Test.

mo. Reporting about the Wolof children of Senegal, Patricia Greenfield and Jerome Bruner (1966: 104) note that those "who have been to school are more different intellectually from unschooled children living in the same bush village than they are from city children in the same country or from Mexico City, Anchorage (Alaska), or Brookline (Massachusetts)." And we hear an echo of this in Inkeles's work (1984: 15) when he says that what he calls the syndrome of modernity can be used "to discriminate between those with more or less education in Mexico, and between those who do and do not listen to news broadcasts in Colombia. . . . It distinguishes . . . within all religions and ethnic groups in Chile, Argentina, India, Bangladesh, Nigeria, and Israel."

Commenting on Maccoby and Modiano's research, Jerome Bruner (1966: 46) says: "If the child lives in an advanced society such as our own . . . he is able to apply the fundamental rules of category, hierarchy, function, and so forth, to the world as well as to his worlds. Let it be explicit, however, that if he is growing up in a native village of Senegal . . . or in a rural *mestizo* village in Mexico, he may not achieve this 'capacity.' Instead, he may remain at a level of manipulation of the environment that is concrete . . . and lacking in symbolic structures—though his language may be stunningly exquisite in these regards."

To recognize features that are common to otherwise different material objects, as the children were asked to do in the equivalence tests, requires the same mental operation as to recognize what two people who hardly know each other have in common. Those who are able to operate in segmented relationships, getting along and communicating effectively with people who occupy different positions or are in different walks of life, are those who can distinguish what is universal from what is personal.

Role segmentation begins with the introduction of school: "The essence of formal education . . . is that one of its principal emphases is on universalistic values, criteria, and standards of performance" (Cohen 1971: 39). Sylvia Scribner and Michael Cole (1973: 556) describe what this means for the learning process: "Informal education fuses emotional and intellectual domains. . . . [In school] what is being taught, instead of who is doing the teaching, becomes paramount. Children are expected to learn by relating themselves solely to subject matter and by disregarding their relationship with the teachers. . . . Schools introduce these universalistic values into traditional societies where particularistic, person-oriented values dominate."

We are now able to understand why middle-class psychotherapists complain about the difficulties of communicating with lower-class patients. It seems that "as a group, the psychiatrists were irritated by the [class V] patients' inability to think in their terms" (Hollingshead and Redlich 1958: 344). According to my reasoning, this happens not simply because of general cultural differences, as has often been suggested, but mainly because lower-class people find it harder than middle-class people to differentiate between the psychotherapeutic relationship and any other; apparently they have not learned to separate out the common purpose of therapist and patient as it differs from their other relationships.

Meanings are conveyed through language. It is easier to make oneself understood, if only superficially, in a person-to-person relationship than to a large audience or in writing. Note, for example, how we use pronouns: in writing, we have to make sure that the pronoun has the right referent. It would not do to write: "When he gave a present to his brother he was very pleased." It is all right to speak this way to a friend, for the listener in a close relationship would "edit" by ear and would understand whether it was the giver or the receiver who experienced the pleasure. But in a universalistic relationship we must speak as if the other person does not know us. Complex role-sets make it impossible to communicate effectively if we assume that everybody is privy to our meanings. I must determine what my listener has in common with me and what the perspective is from his or her position so that I can fashion my communication accordingly. The point is that social structures differ in the extent to which they make demands on individuals to take distance and to sort out what they have and what they do not have in common with others.

Hence, abstract thinking develops where universalistic relationships are salient and where, therefore, goal-oriented behavior can be more effectively structured. In contrast, where particularistic relationships dominate, thought processes are simple in the sense that individuals do not have the opportunity sufficiently to develop the intellectual flexibility needed for a better understanding and for mastering events.

It is interesting to note in passing that, in his empirical study *The Birth of the Gods* (1960), Guy Swanson found that the degree of abstraction and elevation of a society's gods is correlated with the complexity of its social structure (as quoted in Collins 1988: 110).*

Where social relationships are complex—that is, where we have different things in common with people occupying different positions—we are challenged to develop more complex mental abilities. This is to say that *the ability to think conceptually is in large part an attribute of the social structure*. At first sight this statement must be shocking both to those who believe that intellect is an individual attribute and to those who emphasize cultural relativity. Yet, upon further consideration, it should be clear that in everyday language we equate modes of thought with group attributes, as when we call some people "parochial," implying that their limited perspective is due to their belonging to a group that is as closely meshed as a parish, or when we call people "cosmopolitan" in their thinking (Gouldner 1957; Merton 1968b), implying that their orientations feed upon diverse sources stemming from their multiple relationships in their heterogenous environment.

I am well aware of the fact that the statement that the ability to think conceptually is in large part an attribute of the social structure is reminiscent of Lucien Lévy-Bruhl's (1966) concept of primitive logic, and that this notion is anathema in modern social science, especially among relativist anthropologists. Yet the notion is

*Randall Collins's *Durkheimian Sociology* (1988) came to my attention after this book had been substantively written. I am delighted to see that he, unlike social theorists before him, made a point similar to mine about abstract thought as an attribute of a complex social structure. He says that "for members of a highly differentiated modern nation-state . . . symbols charged with social significance are abstract and universalistic." He relates his argument to Durkheim's distinction between mechanical and organic solidarity (cf. my reference to Durkheim in Chapter 3) and also refers to Bernstein's distinction between elaborate and restricted codes in the use of language, as I do in this chapter and in an earlier paper (R. Coser 1975a).

implicit in many empirical studies—even in opinion polls, which find associations between locations and how people think about events. After all, education, especially higher education, is based on the premise that thinking has to be learned, and learning does not take place in a social vacuum. We have heard (from Scribner and Cole, above) that education in schools does not merely consist in the learning of facts and skills; it brings about a separation between intellectual and emotional domains and teaches a new conception of relationships. Among the explanations for learning difficulties among some children who grow up in a so-called culture of poverty, the reason that is usually ignored (Bernstein's [1971] work being a notable exception) is that such children often grow up in an environment that lacks social complexity because of the severe mutual dependency called forth by deprivation. The mammoth study of six cultures by Alex Inkeles and David Smith (1974) finds that the modern person relies, inter alia, on calculability and planning and thinks differently about such things as political events and women's rights.

Tracing the mode and process of thought to the social structure is not so new, after all, if we remember Georg Simmel's (1950) conceptualization of the role of the stranger who, being of two worlds—the world of origin and the present one—is able to develop a sense of objectivity and to understand things that those who are securely embedded in their relationships fail to see. So commonly accepted is this idea that the notion of the "marginal man" first conceived by Ezra Park (1950) has become part of the vernacular. The marginal man, says Park, "lives in two worlds, in both of which he is more or less a stranger" (p. 356). And Park elaborates: "Inevitably he becomes, relative to his cultural milieu, the individual with the wider horizon, the keener intelligence, the more detached and rational viewpoint. . . . It is in the mind of the marginal man that the moral turmoil, which new cultural contacts occasion, manifests itself in the most obvious forms. It is in the mind of the marginal man—where the changes and fusions of culture are going on—that we can best study the processes of civilization and progress" (pp. 376, 356). Park had in mind the modern city dweller. Maccoby and Modiano (1966: 268–69) explain the difference between the traditional village and the modern city: "Unlike the urban world, the small village offers no alternatives to the influence of the family. Even those games by which industrial society teaches reciprocity . . . are not played within the village. . . . Industrialized urban man gains an increased ability to formulate, to reason, and to code the ever more numerous bits of complex information he acquires."

Consider, in contrast, some speech patterns in small societies or in some dyadic relationships. It is no accident that dialects are usually spoken in gemeinschaft communities. A dialect can be "stunningly exquisite," as we hear Bruner (1966: 46) say. People who speak it or have grown up with it call it "charming" and refer nostalgically to the fact that it expresses untranslatable nuances. This is precisely the point: the nuances cannot be raised to the universalistic level. Only when one belongs to the same in-group can one be privy to their meanings.

The language of the small child learning its first words is an extreme example of communication in a particularistic relationship. Only the mother, and perhaps some other family member, can understand that speech. One baby I observed used the word "no more," pointing to an empty glass, to indicate that it wanted orange juice. But it also called a musical record "no more" because it was not playing. This is, of course, particularism in the extreme, in that understanding the communication depends completely on the particular relationship. With such a vocabulary, the child cannot get very far beyond intimates.

Baby talk, as extraordinary as it seems to adults, is a good illustration of restricted speech in an extremely restricted relationship. It reminds us of the distinction I mentioned earlier that Bernstein makes between elaborate speech and restricted speech—such as prevails in a gemeinschaft type of society. In this kind of speech, he says, "the intent of the other person can be taken for granted as the speech is played out against a backdrop of common assumptions, common history, common interests. . . . Often in these encounters the speech cannot be understood apart from the context" (1971: 177). Restricted speech limits relationships to a restricted role-set just as, conversely, a restricted role-set encourages restricted speech, and this ties mental processes to the concrete. Moreover, with the limitation of contacts, opportunities are restricted as well.

Inefficiency of Strong Ties and Restricted Role-Set

I am reminded here of Granovetter's (1973) notion that strong ties are likely to limit opportunities. He demonstrated the ineffectiveness of gemeinschaft ties in the modern world; he analyzed the apparent contradiction between the closeness of relations in the Italian community of Boston's West End and the fact that this community was not strong enough to organize against the urban renewal that ultimately destroyed it. In contrast, another working-class community in the same city successfully organized against the urban-renewal plan. In the first community, social ties were so close that the community's members were hardly encouraged to form outside connections, so they did not have human resources to fight the renewal plan. In the second community, there was a rich organizational life, which meant that roles were segmented; people were in contact with and therefore better able to understand the outside forces that had an immediate impact on their lives.

Similarly, Granovetter (1974: 52–53) showed that there is a "structural tendency for those to whom one is only weakly tied to have better access to job information one does not already have. Acquaintances, as compared to close friends, are more prone to move in different circles than oneself. [In contrast,] those to whom one is closest are likely to have the greatest overlap in contact with those one already knows, so that the information to which they are privy is likely to be much the same as that which one already has."

However, the opportunities offered by a complex role-set are not only those that procure the advantage of information and material resources. It is not only, as Granovetter implies, that the teachers' relationships with the superintendent may get them promotions but that these relationships also force teachers to articulate their roles in concert with other obligations in relation to other role partners, and they thus constitute an impetus to negotiate, to reflect, and to make choices.

It should be clear from what has been said so far that a teacher's relationship to the superintendent of schools is usually not one of choice. Teachers must deal with the expectations of the superintendent whether or not they desire to do so, and even whether or not they have met the superintendent in person. Of course, teachers have a choice as to whether and to what extent they will do the superintendent's bidding, but to some extent the latter's expectations have to be dealt with whichever road one chooses, even if one chooses to reject them; and whatever choice one makes in relation to the superintendent of schools may be at odds with those of colleagues or students. This in turn encourages teachers to weigh alternatives.

A complex role-set is one in which status-occupants *must* deal with role partners who are different in position or outlook than themselves by virtue of their roles, at the same time that they are led to reflect upon their behavior, so that they may have some peace with themselves and with their other role partners. Thus, the concept of role-set sensitizes us to two structural features: the *constraints* imposed by role partners differently positioned in the structure, and, paradoxically as a consequence, the *freedom of choice* these constraints give the individual status-holder. This means that in a complex role-set, where status-holders have to negotiate with several different if not conflicting expectations, their behavior cannot be prescribed in detail. As in a game of chess, behavior depends much on individual assessments of possible moves, and there is simultaneity and interdependence of discipline and freedom.

Pluralistic Structure, Internal Dispositions, and Individualism

In addition to the mechanisms that Merton (1968a: 425–33) has specified as helping to reduce the burden imposed by conflicting expectations of the role partners, it is useful to consider one other that is inherent in the structure of a complex role-set. It derives from Lewis Coser's (1956: 76–81) theory of conflict: multiplicity of conflicts within the role-set helps to prevent polarization into two irreconcilably antagonistic camps. In a complex role-set, the intensity of conflict is reduced by the facts that there are other conflicts and divergences demanding the attention of members of the set and that these conflicts make for different types of alliances on various issues and at various times: "Given segmental participation, the very multiplicity of conflicts in itself tends to constitute a check against the breakdown of consensus" (ibid.: 76). This explains why, as I noted earlier, hostilities and conflicts in a gemeinschaft type of society, in which lack of segmentation minimizes multiplicity of conflicts, can be especially strong. Indeed, if relationships are close, there is a tendency for conflict, whenever it breaks out, to be particularly intense (ibid.: 67).

It stands to reason that both overcommitment and polarizing conflict should be part of the same destructive process. Polarizing conflict marshals strong commitments, divided as they are, of the group's members. In contrast, conflicts that arise from multiple and divergent expectations within people's role-sets help to prevent polarization as well as overcommitment, the two being twin destructive forces for both society and the individual: "In most groups the commitment mechanisms are dampened and inhibited by the interplay of complex and partially inconsistent norms and values of the group and of its environment. Loss of this dampening process leads to a kind of super-commitment in which autonomy, both in moral judgment and role behavior, is replaced by unquestioning obedience, even participating in violence" (Mills 1982).

Lewis Coser (1956) distinguishes between loosely structured and close groups. This is akin to the distinction on the basis of role complexity that Edward Boldt (1978) makes between the looseness and tightness of a society. In an analysis of Hutterite communities characterized as approximating the gemeinschaft type, he uses the distinction I have made between complex and restricted role-sets. He finds:

Where role complexity is limited, individual role players will of course have fewer alternatives that are even potentially available to them. . . . By the same token individuals who are the recipients of imposed role expectation will lack the cognitive preparedness required to avail themselves of whatever alternatives do exist. If this analysis is correct then one would expect the greatest restriction on individual autonomy in those societies that are both tight and relatively simple. (p. 354)

Following upon the work of Ralph Turner (1962) and Ford et al. (1967), Boldt defines a tight society as one in which expectations are imposed and received, as opposed to proposed and interpreted. He quotes Ford: "Where social structure is 'received,' emphasis is on the imperative nature of mores without reference to a legitimizing rationale. . . . Where structure is 'interpreted,' on the other hand, custom is seen as defining *ranges* of tolerable variation rather than the precise content of behavior" (Boldt 1978: 354). This distinction is similar to the one Parsons makes when reading Durkheim to mean that in primitive society "there is a minute regulation of the details of action. With the progress of the division of labor this detailed regulation gradually falls away. The sanctions . . . no longer attach to particular acts . . . but only to very general principles and attitudes" (T. Parsons 1949: 344).

It follows that, using a distinction forcefully made by Merton (1949; 1959), in a gemeinschaft there is more emphasis on *behavioral* than on *attitudinal* conformity. The latter occurs when individuals have strongly internalized values and norms guiding their actions. Behavioral conformity, in contrast, takes place irrespective of attitudes.

In a gemeinschaft, there is little differentiation between attitudes and behavior, and there is little flexibility between them. Values and norms are not strongly internalized, as Boldt (1978) also notes, which means that controls largely remain *external* to the individual. This makes for stronger groups with boundaries, and with well-defined limits imposed on their members' behavior, but it also limits individual choices.

In modern society, the boundaries between groups are fluid, but boundaries have been erected between individuals. While this often exacts the price of estrangement, it is not just a precondition of but is also synonymous with individuation.

One would expect that, where attitudes are most involved in the process of mutual social control, there would be less separation between person and role. Yet the opposite seems to be the case. Individuals can vary their behavior in terms of its appropriateness in different role relationships without these variations necessarily impinging on internal dispositions. Choices between alternatives in behavior do not necessarily alter a person's self-image. In contrast, where role behavior is prescribed and judged according to specific details, there is less awareness of one's own ability to make choices, and "one's own" is a concept that does not enter consciousness to the same extent as in a structure where internal dispositions are relied upon.

This explains at least in part why the legitimation of norms is rarely questioned in a traditional social order. Where specific behavior is the basis of conformity, control comes from outside the person, so that the person does not have to become aware of contradictions. Where it is taken for granted that all women do the feeding and clothing and all men the chopping and hammering, there is hardly any contradiction. Paradoxically, as social control remains primarily external to the individual, the latter experiences himself/herself as a whole. This is because there is no experience of segmentation.

As role expectations are more diffuse, and as attitudes (in contrast to behavior only) are the basis for their allocation and judgment, more decisions are left to the individual. Turner (1962: 23) has noted that "the actor is not the occupant of a position for which there is a neat set of rules . . . but a person who must act in the perspective supplied in part by the relationship to others whose actions reflect roles that he must identify." And Turner and Killian (1972: 60) must have had complex role-sets in mind when they pointed to the individualistic and creative aspects of what they call role-playing: "In playing roles, people are typically engaged in making these roles, sometimes modifying them, sometimes creating new ones."

The separation between the person and the role is the mark of individualism. Ford et al. (1967: 376–77) have expressed this well: "Only when the role-others figuring in one of an individual's role-sets do not figure in others can the individual avoid dependence on one role relationship for the full definition of his identity. . . . It is only where roles are played to a variety of different audiences that the actor can say to one group of role-others: 'I am not only what you think I am. I am also something else.'" This, then, is the safeguard against social greediness.

Individualism thrives under conditions of role-set complexity because such conditions make it possible for individuals to decide whether or not to involve their internal dispositions when they try to conform to the demands of some role partners. And such deliberations are part of the process, just like individualism, of which abstract thinking is a corollary. In a society in which institutions are so differentiated that people can even differentiate their behavior from their internal dispositions, they can develop to its utmost that unique human ability of reflecting about themselves, about their own behavior, and about their thoughts. The better they are able to articulate their consciousness, to weep about and especially to laugh at themselves, the more they will be distinct from the animal world, to which, paradoxically, they continue to belong.

CHAPTER 5

Some Aspects of
Modern Family Structure

The modern family has by and large maintained the features of a gemeinschaft. There is little separation of time and space in the fulfillment of its members' obligations and loyalties. Such separation as exists is an adjustment to the demands that come from the outside and that claim time away from the family, such as work and school. And while the American family adjusts its demands on its members to claims for divided allegiance that come from the outside world, it distributes its own greedy claims unevenly in that it demands priority of commitment from the mother-wife more than from other family members.

The extent to which role segmentation takes place in the family is directly related to the differentiation of activity systems in the society at large and to increased complexities of role-sets. If children learn only from parents, kin, and neighbors, they are completely involved in a gemeinschaft, which controls them as it controls almost all relationships among its members. But the moment there are schools away from home territory, children are expected to leave home in the morning and return at a specified time later in the day. During their absence from home, they are expected to obey a different authority than that of parents, kin, and neighbors. This is one reason, of course, why rural societies have often objected to compulsory education. In other words, authority gets divided by time and space, and other members of the town—say, teachers—also have to segment their lives between home and work, and they exercise a finite measure of authority. Parents will have to adjust to the fact that their own traditional authority over their children has become more limited if for no other reason than that the amount of mutual observability of family members has been reduced.

This applies to some pre-industrial societies as well. We have seen in the previous chapter the difference schooling makes in such societies. It should be noted here that the separation of educational institutions from the family begins to provide some complexity in role-sets. With differentiation of the society there is increased differentiation of time spent with family members and, more important, of time allocated to them. Obligations and rights in the family have to be adjusted to obligations and rights emanating from other institutions.

This introduces restraints at the same time that it introduces choices. In the society inhabited by Leo Tolstoy's (1960) Ivan Illich—a pre-industrial society, to be sure, but one in which there were well-defined professions such as law and medicine—the hero of the story withdraws from his family when his marriage goes sour to devote time and energy primarily to his professional work: "As his wife grew more irritable and exacting and Ivan Illich transferred the center of gravity of his life more and more to his official work, so did he grow to like his work better and became more ambitious than before" (p. 116). In turn, when things at home go well again, he gives less time to his work and concentrates on domestic concerns: "Now that . . . he and his wife were at one in their aims . . . they got on together better than they had done since the first years of marriage. . . . [The work on his house] so absorbed him that his new duties—much as he liked his official work—interested him less than he had expected" (pp. 120–22).

Like a modern person, Ivan Illich makes individual choices between activity systems that determine their range as well as their limitations (Stinchcombe 1975). His alternatives are not unlimited, but he has more choices than he would have if there were not well-delimited activity systems. This separation of institutions presents opportunities for alternative behavior and for their mutual influence on the participation of their members.

In modern society, family members reunite at night and on weekends to rest from the demands of segmented performance—that is, from what they often experience as a fragmentation of self and the burden of multiple role demands. The family provides emotional support and also offers a *claim structure*. Mother or father or an older sibling if there is one (usually in this order) can be called to the rescue. The parents' families of orientation are part of the claim structure: an uncle or an aunt or a grandparent can be called to help out next. Depending on the purpose for which help is needed, the order in which one has a claim on relatives' help is patterned, though flexible. One does not usually call an uncle for help before having called a parent. If a young married person has a flat tire on the road late at night, he or she is likely to call the spouse first. If the latter is ill or absent, he or she would usually call a parent, next an uncle, and only if they are not available will an aunt or a grandparent be approached. Geographical distance is, of course, one factor that may upset this informal pattern.

As I have noted, role segmentation in society at large infringes on the family. Parents have little authority over the children while they are in school, and time is segmented in the children's lives as well. School and extracurricular activities keep the children away from the parents' surveillance. While the mother usually controls the children's schedule, especially when they are young, the whole family has to take account of the fact that everybody is not equally available at all times to work, help, give support, or exercise authority. Occasions for exercising authority and obligations to obey authority are divided in space and time and between people, and so is emotional involvement with the group's members.

Socialization of children is not taken care of by parents alone. As important as the roles of mother and father or parental substitutes may be for the well-being of the individual child and for the child's adaptation to the demands of adulthood, the outside culture is equally important in determining modes of behavior and internal dispositions that may or may not be adaptive. Good examples come from the history of immigration, where whole groups have had to be assimilated into new ways of living and coping. The family is intermediary in this process. But within the family it is not always the parents who take the lead in helping the children to acculturate. Children also help their parents in many ways. Being exposed to schools and peers, they often have more opportunity than their parents to learn and bring home the news of what is and what is not proper or useful. The collective adaptation, or maladaptation as the case may be, of whole groups of immigrants from the same culture results from the interaction of cultural and social-structural forces stemming from both the family and the societal institutions the families come into contact with. Within modern, pluralistic society, families differ in the extent to which they are subject to the intrusion of universalistic patterns on their primary relationships.

Two Types of Family Structure

A comparison of Italian and Jewish immigrant families in the United States* shows that a family structure that does not greatly weaken under the influence of segmented life in the society at large—either because it resists or because it has no access to it—has more of a problem helping its members adapt to that segmented culture, while it has more of a chance to ensure the psychological security of its members through strong solidarity among them.

Anne Parsons (1969) has stated that the Italian family is *centripetal*—that is, its members turn their attention inward. As I read her, she had in mind a comparison with the model of the white Anglo-Saxon Protestant family, which can be seen as a *centrifugal* activity system—that is, one in which the attention of the family members is directed outward, so that intra-family activities have to adjust to the social life outside. Italian families seemed to

*This is part of a study of the social roles of immigrant women that I am conducting under the sponsorship of the Russell Sage Foundation.

Parsons to be concerned with their own family members, subordinating these members' outside activities to the needs of the family and its internal solidarity. The dichotomous concept conjures up the image of one type of family in which the focus of most activities is the family itself, and another type of family in which most activities seem to be oriented outward.

The antonyms "centrifugality" and "centripetality" apply to the difference between Jewish and Italian immigrant families. The contrast can be illustrated by the following true though anecdotal story that I was told during my research. Both Jewish and Italian girls were working in garment shops in New York City. At the end of the working day some Jewish girls stopped for coffee before going home, discussing union activities and potential strike action (as well as gossiping about peers and clothes). Many an Italian girl would have liked to join her Jewish friends but was met at the factory door by a brother who came to escort her home. Southern Italians seem to have had stronger gemeinschaft ties than Jews did. Granovetter's (1973) distinction between strong and weak ties may help to clarify the difference between these two types of family structure.

It seems that Italians have been characterized by their reliance mainly on the strong ties within the family, whereas Jews have been likely to rely more often on weak ties with people outside their families. While everywhere women are more tied to the home than men, this has been even more true in the centripetal Italian family. Of course, the two types of relationships do not represent a clear dichotomy; rather, they are two extremes on a continuum. Even within the same family or kinship group, not all ties are equally strong, nor are all ties outside the family equally weak. Some friendship ties are stronger than some family ties.

In general, the more one reaches outward from the group with which one is identified, the more one is likely to form weak ties; the more one reaches inward, the more one relies on strong ties. Reliance on weak ties is itself, therefore, an index of adaptation to modern society because it points to a group's contact with the external world. To be sure, if there were no strong ties at all holding a group together, this would be a serious sign of anomie. But strong ties among group members are not sufficient for the survival of its members individually or of the group as a group. The fate of some Utopian communities such as Jonestown (Coser and Coser 1979) demonstrates this point.

It will be remembered that Granovetter (1973) has shown that weak ties are the ones that offer opportunities, be it for jobs or advancement or for career generally. I read him to mean that weak ties are more conducive to any kind of opportunity, such as information about the world at large or understanding the health or social security system. In fact, weak ties themselves are opportunities for generating more weak ties, just as capital generates more capital (cf. P. Blau 1977; Bourdieu 1980). Thus it can be said that weak ties are part of a social capital, which may be as important for careers as financial capital.

To say that Italian immigrants are more likely to rely on strong ties does not refer to individual psychological or even cultural propensities. It refers to the composition of the immigrant population. When, at the beginning of the twentieth century, southern Italians came en masse to the eastern seaboard of the United States, they constituted the first southern Italian immigration wave; there was no earlier one that could help in their assimilation.* By contrast, East European Jews who came to the United States at the end of the nineteenth century had been preceded by German Jews who had come shortly after 1848. Not only were the German Jews already settled when the East European Jews started arriving, but they were also of a higher socioeconomic status.

As is well known, German-Jewish Americans were not enchanted with their coreligionists from Eastern Europe, whom they considered coarse, ill-mannered, and uncivilized generally. Yet, a sense of noblesse oblige pervaded the German-Jewish community, which set out to create associations that laid the groundwork for the professionalization of social work (Glanz 1976; Howe 1976). They created the American-Hebrew Alliance, the National Council of Jewish Women, the Hebrew Immigrants Aid Society (HIAS), and others (Baum, Hyman, and Michel 1977:

---

*There was an earlier wave of Italian immigrants, mainly from the north, who went to California (DiLeonardo 1984).

176–79). Through these organizations the Jewish newcomers could get help in getting settled, getting jobs, getting oriented generally—in short, in solving all sorts of problems they faced in the strange country. The antagonism between the two types of Jews, leading to mutual personal avoidance, contributed to the weakness of the ties formed between German and East European Jews. But these ties were stabilized through organizations. Granovetter (1982) makes the point that weak ties must be stable to be effective; otherwise they break down or change into strong ties. Stability, as I understand it, means institutionalization. In creating these organizations, the founders professionalized social work (cf. Glanz 1976) and thus helped stabilize the formation, availability, and at least temporary maintenance of the opportunity for weak ties, not just for individuals but for a whole group. While it is true, as Granovetter also notes, that jobs in modern society are a good source for stable weak ties, these ties are not sufficient to ensure the survival of whole families with children. Immigrants were faced with all sorts of problems that the ties with more or less specialized professionals could solve better than ties between sporadic acquaintances or colleagues on the job. These were problems of settlement, health, citizenship, welfare, and so on. In addition, such professional weak ties could lead to the formation of new weak ties.

A fact that tends to be forgotten is that the social-service organizations I am talking about were founded and staffed mainly by women (Glanz 1976). The clients of these organizations were mostly women as well—the women who represented their families and their families' problems. The ties these women formed through such organizations contributed to the complexity of their role-sets, and this complexity was the source of much of their creativity and individualism. It is to be noted that the ties emanated from the positions the women occupied in the social structure; they were not due to happenstance.

It is useful to consider here the concept of weak and strong ties in conjunction with the concept of role-set, because the latter term refers to role partners who have specific or specifiable positions by virtue of which a person must, or is led to, interact with them. While chance encounters may be useful for the formation of weak ties, even these opportunities are provided by the social structure—if for no other reason than the fact that those who can afford to travel far afield have more opportunities than their poorer counterparts to make new contacts. But random acquaintances are different from people one deals with in one's various activity systems, where most role partners occupy more or less stable positions. Their expectations of the status-occupant derive from these positions: the mother makes demands as a mother, and the teacher expects students to act in a certain way by virtue of their being teacher and students, regardless of their personal styles. As I have noted, having to live up to the various and often conflicting demands emanating from these role partners by virtue of their positions puts pressure on status-occupants to articulate their roles. This demands initiative and often creativity and helps incumbents to become active users of the social structure (cf. Turner and Killian 1972).

Thus the service organizations set up by a wealthier and earlier generation of immigrants, especially the women, were useful not only for the help they provided but for creating a stable network that was an extension of the immigrants' role-sets. They were a source of specific weak ties that were positionally anchored in the social structure.

There were other structural sources of weak ties. A most important one was the social stratification among the new immigrants themselves. Jews came from more varied social classes than did southern Italians, who were mainly *paisani* with a minority of artisans among them. Many Jewish families had both some well-to-do members and some poor ones. Not that the rich always hovered over the poor with protection and help, but this is precisely the point: differences in financial attainment weaken family ties so that, among Jews more frequently than among southern Italians, weak ties existed even within the same families or kin groups.*

* This is a good example of the fact that much of what is usually termed "cultural difference" may well have its source in the social structure. A similar point is made by Evelyn Glenn (1983: 44) in her analysis of Chinese-American families, when she concludes from her research that "distinctly different family types . . . underline the importance of the larger political economic structures in which the family is embedded."

Jewish immigrants were stratified, so there was a significant number of well-to-do who were in a position to provide weak ties for those not so well off. One Jewish immigrant from Russia whom I interviewed about his deceased mother, who had emigrated with her husband and five children, told me how he got his first job in the new country, right after grade school: "My mother knew a Mr. P. in Shul. He had a fur business. She asked him did he have a job for her boy who is the brightest kid ever. He said I should come to see him. He gave me a job sweeping the floor. I stayed there until many years later; when he went broke I took over the business."

Related to the heterogeneous class structure is the broader occupational distribution. I mentioned earlier that the opportunity to form weak ties is unequally distributed in the social structure: the higher the socioeconomic or occupational level, the greater the chance to form weak ties. That is, weak ties are themselves a resource associated with social class. The poor of Tally's Corner in Washington, D.C. (Liebow 1967), as Granovetter (1982) also notes, were hardly able to establish weak ties. On the corner they saw the same people, those with whom they had strong ties but whose experiences for this very reason were the same as theirs and who knew the same things and the same people. In contrast, those who have occupations that are higher on the socioeconomic ladder—physicians, academicians, business people—have many chances to form weak ties.

Professionals, artisans, and entrepreneurs have the opportunity to form weak ties when dealing with clients. Southern Italians who were artisans could form not only some weak ties but complex role-sets as well. Jews frequently were traders. Unlike peasants, who are tied to the land, traders not only have to have clients with whom they have weak ties but also must travel, and traveling affords the opportunity to extend one's role-set. Indeed, among the types of behavior that facilitate the establishment of weak ties, traveling deserves special attention. I have shown elsewhere (R. Coser 1975b) that traveling affords the opportunity of a temporary no-man's-land, a displacement from home and an escape from control by those with whom one has close ties. Traveling may offer opportunities for advancement akin to the frontier.

It is not only that one coincidentally may meet people with whom to strike a deal.* The important thing about the opportunity to travel is that people extend their role-sets.

We know from literature, from anecdotes and jokes, that Jews in Eastern Europe traveled often, even if reality may not have corresponded exactly to nostalgic folklore. Earlier in this book I alluded to the jokes about Jews traveling from Minsk to Pinsk, or Shalom Aleichem's stories about Tevye with his horse and buggy, and about others who defied regulations and trainmasters' controls. Important for our purpose is the symbol of the wandering Jew, eternized by Simmel (1950: 402–8) in his charming essay "The Stranger," who is *positionally* in the habit of forming weak ties. Here today and gone tomorrow, he is part of the group he visits, but not quite. He may derive as much advantage from his partial belongingness as he may be disadvantaged by being an outsider; or he may gain advantage from being an outsider at the same time that he is disadvantaged by having demands he cannot honor made on him by the new group. He may understand the group's shortcomings better than true insiders do, and he may be praised or hated for his objectivity. In any case he will have multiplied his opportunities—be it at the cost of secure belongingness—to form weak ties even with those with whom hostilities are customary. Although much pain ensued from this, advantages came from it as well. Jewish traders made contacts they could use for trading, and, even if it did not provide any other advantages, traveling widened their horizons, taught them the realm of the possible and its limitations, and enlarged their aspi-

*One should not underestimate the opportunities such casual encounters provide. *Science* (March 19, 1982: 1484) reports: "Because Steven Jobs, president and founder of Apple Computer Corporation, happened to sit next to Representative Fortney H. (Pete) Stark (D-Calif.) on a flight from California to Washington last month, one of the largest corporate donations ever made to precollege education may soon take place. During the long journey, Jobs and Stark hatched a scheme that could result in the gift of an Apple computer system to every elementary and secondary school in the United States. The total donation would be valued at $200 million to $300 million at retail prices. In return, Apple would be able to write off a substantial fraction of the cost of the computers against taxes. It would also, of course, score a major publicity coup and ensure that a whole generation of future consumers is introduced to computers in general and Apples in particular."

rations (cf. references to the "marginal man" in Chapter 4; Park 1950). In contrast, one of the characteristics of Tally's Corner is that the men who gathered there did not have the opportunity and hence not the initiative to travel in order to obtain jobs. As Liebow (1967: 44) tells us: "Many of the non-union jobs are in suburban Maryland or Virginia . . . . Public transportation would require two or more hours to get there if it services the area at all. Without access to a car or to a car-pool arrangement, it is not worthwhile reading the ad. So the men do not."

There are also other examples in the sociological literature that show an association between the strength or weakness of ties and the availability or lack of availability of opportunities. In *Street Corner Society*, Whyte (1943: 255–76) asks why Doc, the informal head of a gang of friends, never made it to college, whereas Chick, the head of a club, did go to college. The distinction between the terms "gang" and "club" denotes the differences in the kinds of ties formed among the members. Whyte concludes that the reason for the different careers lies in the fact that Chick did not spend as much time and money on his friends. In contrast to Doc, Chick saved money and did not consider his friendship with his pals a reason for giving all that much of himself. With the help of Granovetter's (1973) conceptualization, we can say today that Chick's much less frequent interaction with club members provided him with weaker ties. He was able to form all sorts of other connections in addition to saving money and having time for schoolwork.

Support for this interpretation comes from another comparison drawn from Whyte's description of the power wielded by some of the people described in his book. I have in mind a comparison between the racketeer Tony and the main protagonist, Doc, the beloved and informally powerful gang leader. Tony commanded power over much of the Italian community. Doc, in contrast, wielded power over his friends in the gang that met at the corner. Tony's power was extensive while Doc's was intensive. Doc's personal power was so strong that, as a result of group pressure, the other boys hardly dared to beat him in a bowling game, whereas Tony had the power to deliver votes to the political machine.

It will be objected that the political machine consisted of strong ties as well. Perhaps this is true as compared with the much weaker ties between, say, patient and physician. I noted earlier that weakness and strength of ties are relative denotations. Some strong ties are stronger than others. A society or group in which all ties are equally strong would be so self-sufficient as to approximate incestual conditions. We must ask what the sources are of ties of some weakness for the southern Italians described by Whyte that made their adaptation possible. One such source (typically not available to women at the time) was the world of politics. Indeed, Tony's ties with the political machine, though not as weak as the ties between, say, a worker and her employer, were still weaker than the ties between Doc and his gang of friends. Hence, Tony had a "big" position in the politics of the North End, a position that Doc could never achieve.

When still in their native countries, southern Italians, just like East European Jews, found themselves in a hostile world, but their positions in relation to that world were so different that they dealt with it in different ways. Southern Italian *paisani* had to make every possible attempt to prevent interference from the outside world. Jews, in contrast, tried to use that world whenever they could. We have known ever since the gripping novels by Ignazio Silone and Carlo Levi that southern Italian *paisani*, in their attempts to liberate themselves from the institutions that subjected them, tried to avoid the schools, the clergy, and the politicians. Jews, who, in contrast to other oppressed groups elsewhere, were never part of the society in which they lived, tried by all possible means to make use of the institutions to which they had only limited access. It was through their ability to form weak ties as a part of their dealings with outsiders that a number of them got access at all. Some such modes of adaptation were formed in their native countries and were then used in their new surroundings, which provided easier access.

Some Theoretical Implications

The question remains: How weak is a weak tie? When does a cousin or an uncle or an in-law constitute a "weak tie"? The strongest ties would be those existing in incestuous groups—a condition, to believe Lévi-Strauss (1949), that makes society impossible (see also Slater 1974). According to Lévi-Strauss, externality is essential for social survival. This contention cannot be proved or refuted, but it is certainly the case that the rule of exogamy, which has it that people ought to marry outside their defined group, serves to extend the role-set consisting of kin and associates.

All societies, primitive or literate, recognize the importance of externality. Esther Goody (1982) has shown that West African societies use the institution of fosterage for the purpose of establishing external ties. In the tribes she studied, those who were successful in their trade or in obtaining political positions were more likely to have been fostered in their childhood. Although fosterage usually, though not always, took place within the kinship system, it provided sufficient ties outside the immediate family for growing youngsters to profit from the opportunities and connections mediated by the foster parents or their descendants. It is interesting to note that fosterage began to take place with strangers in tribes that had become modernized.

Let us come back to the question: How weak is weak? There must be a difference between the uncle who lives in the same household and the uncle who lives a thousand miles away. But a boy's uncle could live in the same city and still constitute a weak tie if there were little interaction between him and the boy's immediate family. If, for example, the uncle had become rich while his sister's family had remained poor, there would be at least some increase in social distance between the two. Such weakened social ties within the same family could be a source of anomie, to be sure, but it would also be a source of opportunity for at least some members of his sister's family through the help he could bestow.

The example of the uncle has been chosen intentionally because of the role uncles, especially maternal uncles, play in many cultures. We know that in Trobriand society, mother's brother exercises authority over her and her children. According to Morris Freilich's (1964) theory of the "Universal Triad," the maternal uncle is the high-status authority in the triangular relationship of himself, father, and offspring; the father is the high-status friend of his children; and the children are the low-status subordinates, as Freilich calls them. In contrast, in the patrilineal and patriarchal society of another South Pacific island group, the Tikopia (Firth 1936; Freilich 1964), the father is the high-status authority and the maternal uncle is the high-status friend. Although these family structures differ in principle, they are similar in one respect, namely from the vantage point of the low-status subordinate. In both types of society, the young person has a taskmaster—the high-status authority—and receives support from the high-status friend. With the help of Granovetter's weak-ties theory and Merton's role-set theory, as well as Esther Goody's theory of foster-parenting, we can now conclude that the maternal uncle, either as a high-status friend or as a high-status authority, is the link (in Granovetter's terms, the bridge) to the external world. Indeed, at the age of about seven or eight Trobriand children leave the parental abode for the maternal uncle's village, where they live in compounds among themselves while they are under his authority. This is structurally similar to Goody's West African children, who are frequently made to leave their parents at the age of six or seven in order to move in with foster parents. It is also similar to the children in U.S. society in the eighteenth century who were sent into apprenticeship with relatives at the age of seven or eight.

Freilich's theory of the triadic relationships between the low-status subordinate and those high-status role partners who use either authority or support makes it possible to add a thought to Merton's theory of role-set. We remember his statement that the difference in positions of role partners in relation to the status-occupant may cause a conflict of expectations for the latter. We can now add that the difference in relationships is not merely a burden. As the cases of Trobrianders and Tikopians illustrate, the young status-occupant derives an advantage in that one of his status superiors—uncle or father—gives him guidance, while the other—father or uncle—gives him emotional support. As I have noted elsewhere (R. Coser 1979), such arrangements prevent the formation of contradictory feelings in relation to the same person; that is, they prevent sociological ambivalence (Merton and Barber 1976).

Moreover, by learning from Freilich and Granovetter, some systematic theorizing becomes possible. Freilich shows that, in

order for the triad to be effective in socializing the low-status subordinate, it is useful for the high-status friend and the high-status
authority not to interact much with each other. In order words,
for the maternal uncle to be effective as a bridge with the outside
world, his relationship with his sister's family should be weaker
than that with his own. Here we have a stable tie that is relatively
weak and that seems to be essential for role-learning, for later
adult performance, and for contact with the external world. For
the sake of theory building, this means that, with the help of Granovetter's (1973; 1982) and Freilich's (1964) conceptualizations and
Goody's (1982) findings, we can now add to Lévi-Strauss's theory
of exchange and alliance with the outside world the fact that the societal obligation of families to generate external ties refers not only
to the choice of mates but also to the socialization of children.

To return to my examples of immigrant families, it is my hypothesis that for southern Italians the godfather (a real or functional uncle) is an institutionalized bridge to weak ties, one that
was perhaps more effective in Palermo or Naples or, better still,
in the hinterland of Eboli (Levi 1947) than in Boston or New
York. By the way, it is interesting to note that during the ancien
régime in France, according to André Bourguière (1980), relationships established with godfathers seemed to have been a bridge
between blood ties and communal bonds. The question arises
whether, in addition to the existence of weak ties, there are resources for people to create new weak ties for themselves and,
further, what the processes and mechanisms are to accomplish this.

With modernization, family ties are often seen as a hindrance
to performance because it is suspected that such ties may override
instrumental considerations in determining decision-making and
policy. This is true for upper-level jobs and for academic jobs,
where the nepotism rule of the past is a good example of the fear
of interference of strong ties. Typically, it does not apply to the
nineteenth-century textile industry studied by Tamara Hareven
(1982), where the use of workers' family ties was a patterned
source of recruitment. In this case the strong ties on the job served
the industry well by preventing geographical and social mobility
of the work force.

Modern society is characterized by a predominance of weak ties, of which those formed on the job are perhaps the prototype in a society where work is separated from the home. But in a primitive society or in other societies not as segmented as our own, ties with people who are less close than immediate family members are probably being established through some other mechanisms.

The more self-sufficient a group is, the less need to form weak ties is felt, and the stronger the ties within the family are. In contrast, the more interdependence between the nuclear family and the outside world, the more the familial ties become weakened. This is what happened to immigrant Jewish families. Since Jews made ample use of American institutions, such as social-service organizations and schools, they developed more weak ties. But this also resulted in a weakening of ties within the family itself. If we learn that, in the same family, sons and daughters belonged to different political parties and that some did and some did not give up their religion (Howe 1976), then this means that their mutual ties became weakened. And if, to boot, they dispersed throughout the country to seek opportunities, their ties weakened further. Eugene Litvak (1985) is right when he says that in modern times family members have continued to stay in touch with each other and to help one another out in many ways. However, this does not mean that family ties are strong. The claim structure may continue to operate among people whose ties are weak enough to be effective in establishing and improving contacts with the external world. As role-sets become more complex and as they include role partners one interacts with only intermittently because of geographical or social distance, ties become weaker even among members of the same family.

Attachments within the same family differ in intensity. In general, women maintain more and stronger kinship ties (Booth 1972; DiLeonardo 1984) and maintain stronger ties within their own family than men do, and mothers maintain, or attempt to maintain, stronger ties than those maintained by grown children. Women who do not work outside the home have less access to weak ties, and their role-sets are generally less complex than those of men. This is because the modern family is still, though less than its traditional predecessors, a "greedy" institution (Coser and Coser 1974). The following chapters will show that women do not have the same opportunities that men have for acquiring weak ties. They usually have a more restricted role-set than men, especially in the middle class.

Part III

· · · · · · · · · · · · · · · · ·

WOMEN

CHAPTER 6

. . . .

Women's Cultural Mandate

The fact that women are supposed to give the priority of their attention to their family of procreation puts them in a premodern role—that is, one in which they do not share the pattern of role differentiation that is customary for modern men. In Chapters 6 and 7 I will explore, first, how the mechanisms for role articulation operate differently for women than for men and, second, what the implications are for gender differences in behavioral patterns.*

Traditionally in modern society men and women have been involved in different activity systems a large part of the day. Until recently, the professions were almost exclusively the realm of men (except for teaching, nursing, and social work), and today women are still tied to the family more closely than men are. The relatively small representation of women in the professions and in high-status positions is a logical consequence of women's cultural mandate, which prescribes that their primary allegiance be to the family and that men be its providers of both economic means and social status. Once the premise of this mandate is granted, women who have or wish to have careers are said to have a "conflict," and this conflict is seen as a source of disruption in the social order.

* This chapter is a revised version of Coser and Rokoff 1971.

The conflict experienced by professional women who have children, and anticipated by young women planning their future, stems not simply from participation in two different activity systems whose claims on time allocation are incompatible. The conflict derives from the fact that the values underlying these demands are contradictory: professional women are expected to be committed to their work "just like men" at the same time that they are normatively required to give priority to their families.

Normative Priorities and Their Routinization

The conflict is one of allegiance, and it does not stem from the mere fact of involvement in more than one activity system. It is a conflict of normative priorities. After all, men are fully engaged in their occupations without fearing, and without being told, that they are not committed to their families. Some will argue that it is precisely this commitment on the part of men that is the driving force for their hard work. Yet one does not think of working men as having a conflict between familial and occupational obligations. It is only when there is a normative expectation that the family will be allocated resources of time, energy, and feeling that cannot be shared with other social institutions that a conflict may arise.

Of course, conflicts of allegiance between the family and other activity systems are not a uniquely modern phenomenon. Economic, political, or religious systems have often competed with the family for the allegiance of its members. There has always been some tension between society's need for the family as a transmitter of status and values to the next generation and society's claim on its members for extra-familial commitments.

In modern society, total allegiance to one or the other activity system is rarely expected. Modern life is, to a significantly greater extent than primitive or medieval life, characterized by individuals' ability to segment their roles. As I have noted in the preceding chapters, the modern person involves some attitudes in some roles, other attitudes in other roles. The most salient roles in modern American society are those of family and work, and normative priorities for involvement are often assigned through prescribed separation of activities by time and place. In my Introduction, I referred to Max Weber's notion that modern capitalism owes much of its tremendously rapid and forceful development to the fact that the place of work became separated from the home (Henderson and Parsons 1947; Weber 1978), and that this has made possible the exclusion of personal needs and desires, of affective attractions and distractions, from the rational pursuit of the efficient enterprise. By combining Weber's notion of the importance of the separation between activity systems with Merton's concept of status articulation, it is possible to spell out the mechanisms that facilitate dealing simultaneously with various status positions. This will also put into a new light the difference between men and women in our society in dealing with their involvements in multiple-activity systems.

I will recap briefly here the formulation of role-sets and status-sets. The term "role-set" refers to the set of role partners who relate to one of a status-occupant's roles. In relation to those role partners, the status-occupant must engage in role articulation if their expectations are incompatible. People have as many role-sets as they have status positions. The total set of role partners in all of a person's status positions is called a status-set, and it is in relation to this set that a person engages in status articulation (cf. Merton 1968d: 423–24).

The separation between the place of work and the home makes it possible for the two role-sets, that of family and that of work, not to overlap; if one role partner accidentally does cross over, as when an associate on the job is also a neighbor, then there is some overlap between role-sets, but still not as much as would be the case if the two realms were not separated. This separation of the different role-sets also makes possible the operation of mechanisms that facilitate and, more important, routinize status articulation—that is, the decision a person must make as to which of the role-sets will be given priority. This is not to say that individuals will never experience contradictory demands in their different roles, but they will face fewer of them than if these mechanisms are not at work.

Through the territorial and temporal separation of activities, the mechanisms of insulation from observability, differential authority over, and differential interest in the status-occupant on the part of various role partners operate more efficiently than if these mechanisms had to be put to work at the same time and place. In this arrangement the individual is insulated not only from observability by the role partners in the other set but also from their authority and their interest. A woman cannot tell her husband how to behave on the job, nor can his employer tell him how to behave at home. The fact that in both cases it can be said that "it is none of their business" bears witness to the normative limits of interest in the status-occupant's behavior in the other system. If it will be objected that men frequently try to tell their wives how to behave on the job, this confirms the point: her being separated from him when she is at work makes the exercise of his authority less likely, if at all possible, in the occupational realm. The formal or informal rule against nepotism, until recently extant in many organizations, is a good example of the custom to separate familial from organizational relationships. This rule, which states that two members of the same family will not be permitted to work for the same employer, has its source in the functional requirement for modern organizations that they remain as much as possible protected from familial concerns and allegiances during working hours. Not only is this to avoid distraction, but it is also a response to the fact that different norms regulate behavior in the different activity systems. If it is objected that the rule against nepotism is obsolete because in complex modern organizations the internal separation of offices and lines of command insulates individual members of the same family, this confirms the usefulness of the separation between different areas of activities in ensuring insulation from observability as well as involvement in a different authority structure. This at least reduces, if it does not eliminate, the potential conflict.

The important fact about the operation of the mechanisms for role articulation is that they reinforce the normative pattern of priorities, which helps remove from individuals the burden of making their own decisions anew in most situations. Thus expectations concerning everyday behavior become largely routinized. Children learn early that there is no choice in the matter of leaving home in the morning for school; no decision has to be made as to whether or not adults are to go to work. This routinization accounts for the fact that the various activity systems operate relatively smoothly even as they demand criss-crossing allegiances from their participants.

It would seem that the mechanisms for dealing with multiple allegiances operate in the same way for men and women. Yet this is not always the case. These mechanisms are a necessary but not a sufficient condition for routinizing status articulation. They are likely to eliminate the conflict only when they help status articulation become routinized, and this happens under conditions of normative consensus about priorities. It is because the expectation that the father be at work during the day and children at school is shared by all that no decision has to be made about whether and when to take up these activities. Where normative consensus is lacking or where there is normative ambiguity, as is still the case today for mothers who work outside the home and have young children, the routine is likely to break down often enough to cause strain in the system.

Emergency situations are a convenient example of occasions when the routine breaks down. The way emergencies are handled in the family, whether or not women go out to work, indicates the difference in normative priorities for men and women, thus highlighting the fact that the mechanisms for routinizing status articulation fail to operate for women the way they do for men.

The Failure of Routines and Status Articulation

To consider something an emergency is making a claim for interruption in the routinized distribution of activities. An emergency occurs when one activity system claims the time and effort that are normatively assigned to the other, as when a mother or father has to stay home from work to care for a sick child or has to work on a weekend instead of being available to the family. In such instances of unanticipated demands—that is, when the demands cannot be dealt with through ordinary normative regulation—an individual has to articulate his or her status anew by making a decision about which of the status-set's demands will be given priority.

However, such a choice is not between equally weighted alternatives. In all likelihood it will be the mother, not the father, who will stay home for the sick child, and it will be the father, not the mother, who will give to the job the weekend time usually assigned to the family. The choice between two activity systems follows a preferential cultural pattern. The woman has the cultural mandate to give priority to the family. Even when working outside the home, she is expected to be committed to her family first, her work second, and this helps prevent disruptions within the family.

Nonroutinized status articulation, even if it does not violate the norm, is potentially subversive. The working woman's expected commitment to her family is considered a potential source of disruption in the occupational sphere because "those involved in the role-set have their own patterned activities disturbed when [the status-occupant] does not live up to his role-obligations" (Merton 1968d: 436). This is likely to happen even if the mechanisms operate or are manipulated to maximize the status-occupant's insulation from observability by the role partners and from the exercise of their authority and interest. Incompatible expectations force the individual to articulate the status anew, to give priority to some normative demands at the expense of others. The woman who remains absent from work in order to care for a sick child creates a disruption in her place of work; the father who cannot come home for dinner because of some emergency at work creates a disruption at home. *Implicit in the act of articulating one's status beyond the routine is a disruption within one role-set, whether or not the disruption is considered legitimate.*

Role articulation tends to be more disruptive when a person

must deal with several role-sets by virtue of his or her various status positions. This situation is more likely to involve a choice between two spatially distinct places at one and the same time, thus increasing the risk that a whole separate role-set will be abandoned when the role incumbent decides to turn to the other set. But this means that for women the very arrangement that facilitates routinized role articulation—territorial and temporal separation between activity systems—makes manipulation more difficult when a status has to be articulated anew, as happens in emergency situations. The separation between home and work does not give a wife-mother the same advantage it gives a husband-father, because if she works outside the home she is still not free from the cultural mandate of being devoted to her family first. The separation makes it more difficult for the mother to combine her gainful work with her household activities and thus to alternate between the two and "cheat" one or the other without much notice. Such is the constraint of her cultural mandate that just because the two systems are separated in time and place, it is harder for the mother, but not for the father, to live up to simultaneous demands emanating from the two activity systems.

Role articulation is easier to achieve when the cultural mandate concerning priorities is unequivocal, because the mechanisms of insulation and of differential authority and interest favor the routinization of activities. If, however, the cultural mandate is equivocal—that is, if a person is expected to give priority to the place of work at the same time as having to be committed to the family first—then routinization breaks down and the separation between the two activity systems makes status articulation most difficult; it is this, rather than the scarcity of time, that produces role conflict. Individuals anticipate the disruptions they might create in situations that would demand repeated status articulation. The conflict about priorities and about whether or how to manipulate the mechanisms for role articulation is structural, not only in the sense that it stems from incompatible or contradictory demands but also in the sense that individuals anticipate that status articulation will create some disruption for someone in the role-set. The conflict is not merely their own; it is between two activity systems, each of which makes legitimate demands on the actor's allegiance.

One reason why women's involvement in gainful employment outside the home has been such a hard nut to crack is that the anticipation of such structural role conflict creates social anxiety, which in turn helps activity systems remain protected from disruptions. There is a fit between the perceived need of potential recruits to occupations to minimize the conflicts that would ensue from repeated demands for status articulation and the alleged need of occupations and professions to minimize disturbances resulting from such status articulation. This often induces women to limit their options by *wanting to do what they have to do* and legitimizes discriminatory practices in occupations and performance, thus narrowing women's access to opportunities.

The Cultural Mandate

If, before the successes achieved by the women's movement, women had pressed for admission to medical schools and law schools and academic disciplines the way Jews used to, they would have crashed the gates much earlier than they did. The reason they did not is that women tended to accept the cultural mandate in defining their own priorities as belonging to the family. This was more true in the past than it is today (Mason et al. 1959). At the time, 87 percent of the nursing students in Fred Davis and Virginia Oleson's (1965) study ranked "devotion to family" first among their choices between this item and "attractiveness to men," "activity in community affairs," and "dedication to work and career." The reason for this choice lies in the most familiar of all facts: that almost every woman is married or hopes to be married. The family is the locus of consensus regarding the cultural mandate.

The most salient value that has pertained to women's cultural mandate is that they ought to expect men to be the main providers of economic means and of prestige. Erik Grønseth (1970, 1971) considers this the most important source of gender inequality. It accounts for the fact that, although the nature of all the pressures deterring women from planning careers still awaits systematic investigation, women learn all through their early lives at home and in school, and later in college, that their value commitments differ from those of men. The woman is to be the caretaker of the family, whose prestige is determined by a man, a fact testified to by her taking her husband's surname and by the stigma attached to the woman who is said to be a spinster.

Sex segregation in school in regard to physical activities and the emphasis on masculine prowess are perhaps not as symbolically important in teaching women their "proper place" as the fact that it is the boys who will give public prestige to the school through their performance in games and it is the girls who are to act as cheerleaders. This is the general image of women's role: they are to cheer men on, to help men in *their* achievements.

The popular film *M.A.S.H.* (1970) offered a good example of this cultural message. One of the principal characters is a professional military woman, a nurse, on the surgical ward of an army base. She is shown to overconform to military norms and to repress her sexuality. However, her sexuality emerges as a form of entertainment for the whole base as her awkward lovemaking is broadcast over the camp loudspeaker. Later, her nude body is exposed to the cheers of the professional male crew. At the end, when the conflict that is the main plot of the movie gets resolved through the all-American, consensus-producing device of a ball game, she finds true happiness as a cheerleader.

Although today it has become acceptable for women to seek careers, there is still a negative connotation to the term "career woman." No such derogatory term exists for men, since their careers are taken for granted. Even today it is still acceptable, even commendable, for a middle-class woman to take a job to help her husband advance his career by going to school, or to help children go to college. Her caring in this way for members of the family is seen as part of her cultural mandate.

As a corollary, women are available to pick up the slack at times and places where an occupational system gets overloaded—that is, when it does not want to allocate resources that are considered too costly for an activity that nevertheless has to be carried out. Women's availability for such jobs stems, of course, from the fact that home and family do not need all the time at their disposal. They can fill in as salespersons (still today often called sales*girls* no matter what their age because of the low status of the activity) at Christmas time; be invited on the spur of the moment to teach introductory courses when an unexpected high number of freshmen enter a class; be called upon when a college department has to give service by teaching what is defined as "unessential" courses (say, sociology to students in nursing, engineering, or business); or serve as volunteers in understaffed hospitals, where they are supposed to make up for the lack of nurturing services— implying that nurturing is an unessential activity, something that is nice when you can get it but that we cannot afford to allocate valuable (i.e., paid) time to. Paradoxical as it may seem, women's time is considered cheap precisely because they live up to the highly prized cultural mandate. This is because, it will be remembered, it is the occupational role that gives prestige, and prestige-seeking is mainly assigned to men (whose prestige, by the way, is, of course, served by their wives' volunteer and entertainment activities. See Papanek 1973).

What is at stake is that women are not supposed to be equal to men, much less superior, in their talents and achievements. The mass media often show women to be smarter, but if they are truly smart, they will manipulate the situation so as to make men believe that they, and not the women, have ultimate control. It is still true that, for this reason, according to my experience with students, many educated and talented women do not attempt to enter or be trained for high-status professions. This is why, in spite of the increases of women in the professions, by 1980 they constituted less than 14 percent of lawyers and of physicians (13.8 percent and 13.4 percent, respectively; *Statistical Abstracts* 1985). We learn from the *Interim Report of the Task Force on Women, Minorities, and the Handicapped in Science and Technology* (1988: 36) that "despite continued career gains, women have not been choosing careers in science and engineering in the same proportions as in the nonscientific professional and managerial areas. . . . In 1985 women were only 13 percent of all college and university science faculty and 2 percent of engineering faculty."

Even when some modern movies seem to convey the manifest message of the "new woman," career and family life have been presented as mutually exclusive alternatives for women, as in *Turning Point* (1977) and *Kramer v. Kramer* (1979). An image is presented of modern women who are less capable than modern men in segmenting their various roles and statuses. The American family appears as a "greedy institution," which demands the total allegiance of women.

It now becomes clear why women are hard put to avail themselves of the mechanisms of status articulation to the extent that men do. Status articulation between two activity systems is rarely routinized for working women with children because the family too often claims time and energy from them that is expected to be assigned to work. The normative priorities for working women who have a family are ambiguous: if they live up to the normative requirement of caring for their families in situations of unexpected demands (such as illness), then they introduce a disruption in their place of work; if they do not live up to this normative requirement, then they introduce a disruption in the family.

The anticipation of conflict this creates in women is integrated with the desire on the part of organizations to prevent disruptions as they are socially defined. These two factors account in large part for the still unequal representation of women in high-status positions and in the professions.

The Opportunity Structure

The largest proportion of working women are to be found in lower-status occupations.* This seems contrary to the claim that type of employment of women is related to their family commit-

---

* However, women are hardly to be found on the very lowest level. Shoeshine boys and garbage collectors, for example, are men. Similarly, some working-class occupations that require what is culturally defined as "masculine" work are practically closed to women, such as truck-driving and mechanical work of all kinds.

ments. For it seems curious that women should be fairly well represented in occupations where the day is long and the hours are rigidly controlled, and that they are not well represented in professions where they can more readily manipulate their allocation of time. Would it not seem that women would be less likely to cause disruptions in a type of work that does not so much depend on regular presence for the major part of the day? The woman physician in private practice could decide to practice only part of the day or to have office hours at night; the woman college teacher could do much of her work evenings and weekends—her presence at school is not strictly required except for meetings and scheduled classes. Yet women are more likely to be found in occupations that demand a full day's involvement and where there is little flexibility for the manipulation of time, and they are less likely to be in occupations in which they could follow a flexible schedule. This would seem to contradict the earlier statement that the sex distribution in occupations is to be understood in terms of minimizing disruption resulting from competing allegiances. For it should stand to reason that occupations that can follow a flexible schedule can absorb the shock of disruption more easily than those that depend on rigid time-keeping, and that women would be attracted precisely to occupations where they can manipulate their time and hence more easily articulate their status.

The difference between occupations in which women are well represented and those in which their participation is conspicuously rare seems to be that, irrespective of the requirements of schedule, most women are in occupations in which each individual worker is *replaceable, or defined as replaceable*, and they are less likely to be in occupations that are seen as demanding full commitment allegedly based on individual judgment and decision-making.

What is important here is not so much the technical nature of the task as the social fact of normative requirements. High-status positions are said to require the commitments necessary for exercising individual judgment. In those positions people allegedly control their own work; they are said to be in charge of defining its nature so that hardly anyone else can do it for them. One recognizes here the definition of unalienated labor. If Alice Rossi

(1964) bemoans the fact that American women tend not to engage in "meaningful" work, this is exactly the point: it is not that women are not expected to work; it is only that they are not expected, in the same way men are, to be committed to their work through their individual control over it. If they were so committed, it is feared that they would subvert the cultural mandate, thereby allegedly causing disruption in the family system, and would risk being seen as disrupting the occupational system as well.

Replaceability and Commitment

Replaceability on jobs where women are or feel readily admitted, as well as commitment to and individual control over work in which they are or feel unwelcome, are, to be sure, not inherent in the nature of the work. That we deal here with social definitions of replaceability and commitment rather than with actual task requirements can be shown by two examples: the social definition of replaceability in school teaching, which is done mainly by women, and the social definition of individual control over patients in a hospital by the predominantly male house staff.

In schools there is an institutionalized mechanism for allowing absenteeism. The prediction that there will be a high rate of absenteeism among teachers, who are predominantly women, has led to a separate suboccupation, that of substitute teacher (in nursing, the equivalent is the floater), for which, in many states, a special diploma is needed. Everyone knows, however, that substitute teaching is a poor substitute for teaching. Notoriously the students are hostile to substitutes, and their hostility is patterned in that it is tolerated by adults and expected by peers; hardly anybody expects that pupils will learn much while their teacher is off the job. Surely, if we examine the nature of teaching, we recognize that a grade school teacher has as much control over the class as a college teacher and should, therefore, be just as irreplaceable if not more so. Yet, what seems to be important is to prevent the disruption in the system that would occur if pupils were left unattended or if the already overloaded classrooms were required to double up. Substituting in teaching does not serve to replace performance as much as it serves to avoid disruption.

Let us consider, in contrast, a higher-status profession like medicine. Here, the work is defined as personal service to the patient. Although, as far as the nature of work is concerned, interns and residents on a hospital service could replace one another because they usually know one another's patients, residents, whether male or female, will not make use of this de facto replaceability by giving priority to the demands of their family. The house staff is supposed to learn during training the importance of individual responsibility for and control over individual patients, with all the commitment this entails. This explains at least in part the disproportionate demands made on the trainees' time and energies in teaching hospitals. Here, absence due to anything other than serious illness or death in the immediate family is out of the question. In this normative system, the ethos is that there be no priority of commitment to the family on the part of man *or* woman. Consequently, there are relatively few women in this profession, even though their number has significantly increased in recent years.

Occupations differ in the measure of the commitment they claim from their members, and this measure is directly related to prestige in the stratification system. The distinction noted in Chapter 4 between behavioral and attitudinal conformity (Merton 1959) can be usefully applied here. In routinized occupations, performance requires mainly *behavioral* conformity to detailed prescriptions and little involvement of internal dispositions. Professionals, by contrast, are to be guided by *attitudes* and internal dispositions, and leeway exists concerning behavioral details (R. Coser 1966). Individual decisions regarding courses of action are to be made, and if these are to conform to standards, then they must be informed by internalized values on which to rest individual judgment. Between the two extreme expectations of pure behavioral and pure attitudinal conformity lies a continuum of relative emphasis on either type, determined by the measure of routinization and the measure of individualization of judgment and control that are allegedly involved in the practice of a particular occupation. For example, grade school teaching and nursing should require attitudinal involvement; yet to the extent that these occupations are socially defined as being routinized, there is less expectation of internal involvement and the practitioners are considered to be replaceable in their work.

Commitment can be defined as the positive involvement of internal dispositions, but it is useful to make a second distinction, namely, between commitment to one's *work* and commitment to *other persons* engaged in the same work. In high-status occupations, commitment is expected to be not only to work but to one another. It is important not only that the work be done but also that it be done with the approval of colleagues with whom one shares basic values (Bosk 1979). Long years of training serve not only to teach technical skills but also to instill the necessary attitudes and professional values (Merton 1957). The future commitment and the strength of the bonds of solidarity with co-professionals are to be commensurate with the investment of time, energy, and emotion that such long years of intensive training require. Co-professionals are to become a particularly meaningful reference group toward whom the practitioners' internal dispositions will be oriented. All through their training, "the theme is mutual commitment, reinforced by students' auxiliaries sponsored by the professional associations, and by the use of such terms as 'student-physician,' which stress that the student is already in the professional family. One owes allegiance for life to a family" (E. Hughes 1963).

And thus allegiances are sex-typed: a man owes to his profession what a woman owes to her family.* An occupation that requires the involvement of internal dispositions demands the kind of absorption of the mind that the family claims from mothers and wives. The writer Marya Mannes (1963: 125) points to a woman's deep involvement: "No woman . . . can compose a paragraph

*Harry Hall (1966), quoting from hearings before the U.S. Senate Subcommittee on Military Affairs in 1945, stated that "[a characteristic] of scientists was their intense commitment to the ideals and pursuit of science. 'I have personal knowledge of several scientists who stayed in the work almost entirely because of the love of the work rather than the salary that they received.'"

when her child is in trouble or her husband ill: forever they take precedence over the companions of her mind." Although this seems somewhat exaggerated today when an ever increasing number of women have proved that their deep commitment to their professions can no longer be denied, it is still true that in general women are more involved than men are when a member of the immediate family is ill or otherwise in trouble. As Epstein (1970: 976) notes, the commitment of "women professionals [who] do not or cannot work the same number of hours as their male colleagues . . . is suspect, and they are not deemed colleagues in the full sense of the word."

The type of commitment that is ideally expected of the professional implies selflessness and devotion to a calling. It brings to mind the stereotypical image of the traditional country physician who forgoes sleep and food to ride through the night in snow and mud in order to save lives; or the traditional priest who forgoes the comfort of a family to save souls; or the scientist who forgoes monetary gains for the love of research. This kind of devotion, even if it exists mainly as nostalgic imagery, commands prestige. And this is why, as a consequence, prestigeful positions are said to require commitment.

Since women are expected to give this kind of commitment to their families, they tend to be restricted to the type of work that is defined as requiring a larger measure of behavioral conformity and a smaller measure of attitudinal involvement (cf. Merton 1949; 1959); this designates them mainly for the type of employment where they are replaceable in case of disruption caused by their normative family commitment.* The distinction between routinized tasks and professions also applies to the stratification system. The lower the status, the more it is associated with expectations for behavioral conformity (cf. Kohn 1963; 1975). The higher the status, the more it is said to require the involvement of internal dispositions, and the less it is defined as being replaceable.

*In regard to commitment being associated with maleness and high status, see Davis and Oleson (1963). On value orientation toward—as well as occupational requirements for—behavioral conformity among blue-collar workers, see Kohn (1969b; 1975).

As a result, professions that are sex-typed as feminine will be accorded less prestige. A corollary of the principle of replaceability is that a profession in which women predominate will be defined as requiring less commitment, whether or not it does, or at least could profit from it. Although grade school teaching and nursing can be said to need much attitudinal involvement, the premise of the cultural mandate depresses the commitment value of these occupations and hence depresses their prestige. This is, of course, only a restatement of the familiar fact that women have lower status than men in the culture at large, and this is carried over to female occupations in the public image. As a consequence, professions try to protect themselves lest too many women in their ranks depreciate their prestige with the public. The reluctance, until relatively recently, of medical schools to admit women students is similar to their reluctance in a still earlier day to admit Jews. At that time, for a profession to be typed "Jewish" was as derogatory as it still can be today to be typed "female."

It would seem that strong commitments are held to be incompatible with disruption of activities. Yet it will be objected that professionals and other high-status occupants cause disruptions when their commitments take them away from their place of work. This raises the problem of legitimate and illegitimate disruptions.

Legitimate Disruptions, Role Flexibility, and the Self-Fulfilling Prophecy

In high-status positions, provisions exist for disruptions and for flexibility of role performance. These provisions are not equally available to men and women.

If high-status occupants were to stay put at their desks, they would resemble employees at the lower levels of bureaucratic structure. In actual fact, high status is associated with demands emanating from many places. The chief of a teaching hospital, for example, has to go to meetings all over the city or region and participate in regional, national, and sometimes international meetings, not counting trips to Washington and elsewhere in the country to give counsel. Professors travel to give lectures elsewhere, take part in conferences, give consultations, and every so often take a leave of absence for a semester or a year. These absences create disruptions in their organizations. The hospital's chief is often absent from rounds, staff meetings, and case conferences. A professor may have to cancel classes, and advanced students may be left without a thesis advisor.

With rise in status, the number and diversity of obligations as well as the number of role partners increases, and this multiplies the number of expectations. Correlatively, the more complex the role-set, the more territory it covers. This augments the demands for being in many places, because the commitment of professionals is not only to their work but to one another, and colleagues are scattered all over the country, if not all over the world. Consequently, the higher the status, the more likely that all obligations cannot be met. The rule enunciated earlier—that the higher the status, the less is the position defined as being replaceable—must be supplemented with another rule: the higher the status, the more frequently will demands upon its occupant cause disruptions at work.

It seems paradoxical that women should tend to be unacceptable in positions where commitments to the family might cause disruptions when disruptions seem to be taken for granted in high-status male occupations; more than that, high-status occupants, especially when they are male, are usually congratulated for bringing honor to the organization by being wanted elsewhere.

Disruptions caused by familial demands on women (and sometimes, but rarely, on men) are not considered legitimate because they are seen as being due to a *failure* to meet occupational expectations. In contrast, disruptions caused by professional demands on men (and sometimes, but rarely, on women) in high-status positions are deemed to be legitimate because they are seen as being due to *fulfillment* of occupational expectations.

This kind of discrimination does not concern family involvement as much as it concerns social status. Since in American culture generally women are considered to be of lower status than men, this affects their professional and organizational life. Professional women are usually in situations of contradictory status—a condition about which Everett Hughes (1971a) has written eloquently. They do not always enjoy the same prerogatives as men of similar status. For example, the organizational flexibility built into expectations of performance in high-status positions does not always exist for women. Lotte Bailyn (1984: 81–82) reports the following story:

> When a young faculty member in a major university complained to the dean about the department chairman, the reply was: "Don't be so hard on him, he just got a divorce." The faculty member was amazed. She herself had just had a baby and held an administrative position on top of her full-time teaching schedule. No one, she felt sure—least of all herself—would have excused any lax behavior on her part on personal grounds.

Generally, men, especially when they have high status, are more easily granted what has been called idiosyncrasy credit (Hollander 1958), being permitted some deviance by showing otherwise prized qualities (L. Coser 1967), like the famous professor who is free to cancel classes more often than his less famous colleagues.

It is not only that some measure of deviance is tolerated from high-status occupants, but also that they are often congratulated for showing that they take their status lightly by deviating from a strict adherence to its demands (cf. R. Coser 1966; Goffman 1961). This raises the more general problem of legitimate and nonlegitimate flexibility of role-performance.

Concern with extra-professional issues may testify to the fact that the status-occupant is not *narrow*. If a man of high status takes time out to show concern for his family, he gives evidence of being a good family man, a trait highly prized in a man who has a responsible position. As long as his attitudinal conformity cannot be questioned—and the likelihood of not having it questioned is directly associated with the prestige his status commands—occasional disruption is permitted and may even call forth approving smiles from role partners, as, for example, when the male executive announces in his office that he must take time off to buy his wife a valentine. This would not be so readily tolerated in a woman, who would be accused of neglecting her job for her family. Flexibility for the holders of high status, especially if they are men, is welcome in bureaucratic organizations because it helps to lower status boundaries. If persons of high status deviate somewhat from their obligations, they imply that they renounce some claims on status prerogatives. In contrast, lower-status occupants, who have fewer prerogatives, have fewer resources from which they can offer something in return for taking the license of deviating from the norm.

For professional women it is more risky than for men to openly articulate their family status. The following conversation, as recorded in my field notes, took place between two faculty members and illustrates this point:

> *Professor X to Professor Y*: I think that Joan [who is now only giving an introductory course] should be given a position in the department. She is a good teacher and does good work.
> *Professor Y*: I don't think so. The other day after classes I said to her: "We should have a conference about our next year's program. Can we talk about it now?" And she said, "No, it's too late, I have to go home because the children are home from school." She is just not committed as a professional.
> *Two days later, Professor X to Professor Y*: We should have a meeting because the deadline for next year's curriculum is drawing close. How about meeting this afternoon, since there are no classes?
> *Professor Y*: I can't today, I have to go home to baby-sit.
> *Professor X*: That's good of you. Perhaps we can meet tomorrow.

Although both Joan and Professor Y have disrupted the relationship with a role-partner by giving priority to parental obligations, only Joan is accused of lack of commitment to her work. In contrast, Professor Y—a male—is congratulated for taking time out for his family.

Women's occupational status is never quite legitimate. Since women, even if they are professionals, tend to share the values that assign them to the family, they often feel guilty about "intruding" in the world of men (Strotzka 1969). Whether they are actually considered to be intruders or merely fear being so considered, this may lead them to a kind of overconformity (much emphasized in the mass media) that is reminiscent of the lower-class person who insists on respectability. Those who are not fully accepted sense that they meet with less tolerance than those who are. This explains J. E. Dittes and H. H. Kelley's (1956) findings in their small-group experiments that individuals who felt accepted in a group felt free to express disagreements publicly, while those with a low sense of acceptance were much higher in their public conformity (see also Menzel 1957). If people in secure positions make a display of flexibility or even nonconformity, they show permissiveness. In contrast, if people in insecure status positions want to be flexible, they arrogate for themselves a freedom they have not been given the right to claim. While women who insist on status prerogatives appear to be aggressive, they appear similarly aggressive if, by permitting themselves flexibility, they make a claim for immunity—a claim they are not readily granted. In our culture it is understood that, if a woman has a family, it should command her major commitment, and this could cause a detriment to her occupation. Yet, if she is single, she is "deviant" and is looked down upon for not having been able to attract a husband. If she is single and still young, she may yet succeed in finding a husband, in which case it is predicted that her career will be jeopardized. This is not acknowledged as freely today as it was in 1970, when a faculty member from a prestigious university, who prided himself on his liberal views, had this to say: "The chairman of my department refuses to give fellowships to women. He has a point. It's a bad investment. When they marry or have children, they drop out" (Coser and Rokoff 1971).

This is the process of the "self-fulfilling prophecy" (Merton 1968d: 475–90) by which opportunities are so structured that women will be less likely to be trained and, if trained, less likely to be employed in high-status positions than men with equal potentialities for achievement. This process also accounts for the fact that even today women are often actually encouraged to drop out before getting their degrees. Or, many young women are likely to anticipate much earlier in life that marriage and children will make it difficult to use the qualifications they could acquire, and they therefore refrain from seeking training commensurate with their abilities.

Still today women are being discouraged from partaking in

the complex structure of role relationships in the same way as men. The fact that they are made to anticipate a conflict between the two activity systems of home and career encourages too many of them to withdraw from the role complexity that modern life has to offer.

This raises an important theoretical question. In this book I have argued that role and status articulation imply choice. However, I must add—as is implied in Merton's theory—that choices are made available within an externally given structure. Options are not equally weighted, for some alternatives are more culturally acceptable than others. As Arthur Stinchcombe (1975: 16) notes, "The social process presents a socially structured choice between alternative cognitive styles. People do choose among cognitive styles in order to make history, but . . . they do not make history as they please."

Epstein (1987) bemoans the public concern with women's role conflicts between combining careers and domestic life. She seems to say that this definition of the situation is *only* in the mind. To be sure. But it is the cultural mandate of traditional women's roles that legitimizes both the public concern and women's acceptance of it. Epstein found that successful women lawyers did not suffer from role strain, even those who were trained in the 1960's, when the profession "typically defend[ed] itself against threats . . . , against the inclusion of women in its ranks" (p. 26). But it is to be noted that such women must remain exceptional as long as, to paraphrase Stinchcombe, externally constraining facts get into people's minds (p. 16). True, "the objection to women 'having to do it all' is really an objection to women 'having it all'" (ibid.). I could not agree more that this is the latent function of this public concern. Yet employers who refuse to hire women because they fear that their commitments to the family will create a disturbance are not aware of this latent function, by definition. I have personally witnessed at a committee meeting two men almost coming to a fistfight over the issue of whether one has the right to bar a woman from employment when she intends to have a child. And women have in large part internalized the legitimacy of this concern. The universal emphasis on the cultural mandate for women, the social definition of the conflict between the culturally mandated role and any other a woman might select, exercises a pull on individual decisions toward the culturally preferred mode.

In every society, and especially in an open society like the United States, there are forces that pull in another direction. This is not the place to list them. It should only be noted that college life helps to crystallize available options in that it highlights contradictory expectations college women face. Among the college women whose role conflicts Mirra Komarovsky (1974) has so dramatically described, many ended up in professional careers—and some of them may well have become the respondents in Epstein's study. Today, as Epstein also shows, such women are no longer so exceptional. It is easier for a college woman today to articulate for herself a role as a future professional than it was in the 1950's or 1960's. "As the structurings of choice change . . . so the rates of choice change" (Stinchcombe 1975: 17). The pull of the cultural mandate is not as strong as it used to be.

Nevertheless, women are still being encouraged from childhood to accept the cultural mandate. This does not mean that what happens in early childhood predetermines a person's development for life. But it does mean that at every stage of development a person faces cultural definitions of the situation that have been prepared for at a previous stage. Even now, as countervailing messages are being heard loud and clear, as girls and women are being made to face the contradictions more self-consciously than ever before, as expectations become more flexible, and as women's motivations as well as external pressures are changing, the cultural mandate for women to be committed to the family first has not changed much in its manifestations*—from watching mother in the kitchen to being excluded from boys' games to being told that mathematics is not for girls and that girls must stay close to home. Some implications of this will be examined in the next chapter.

---

*For an excellent piece of research on this topic, see Arlie Hochschild (1989).

CHAPTER 7

. . . .

Women's Use of Space

> In Luciania, when a boy is born, a pitcher of water is
> poured into the road to symbolise that the newborn
> baby's destiny is to travel the roads of the world.
> When a girl is born, water is thrown on the hearth to
> show that she will lead her life within the walls of the
> home.
>
> —Elena Gianini Belotti, *Little Girls*
> (as quoted in Ward 1978: 152)

The implications of women's cultural mandate are
far-reaching. One consequence of what has been
said in the preceding pages is that women are supposed to stay
close to home. Some of the responses of the elderly immigrant
women who were interviewed for my study (see Chapter 5) to the
question "Would you describe your idea of a good wife?" are certainly not typical of modern wifehood but are a dramatic, if anti-
quated, illustration of traditional homeboundedness. We hear that
"a good wife has to stay home." One respondent referred to herself: "I used to be home all the time." Another one was more explicit: "My husband wanted a wife that would be home when he
got home." Although contemporary American women are a long
way from these traditional immigrants, their practices are still
with us in the extent to which girls and boys, women and men,
move away from home.

Environmental variables that have not yet been sufficiently ex-
plored in regard to gender differences are those of the differential
use of physical and social space.* The latter refers to the different

---

*For an earlier version of this chapter, see R. Coser 1986.

social structures in which boys and girls, men and women, play out their social roles. I believe that not only "human development" generally, as Urie Bronfenbrenner (1979: 59) tells us, but also cognitive development in particular are "facilitated through interaction with persons who occupy a variety of roles and through participation in an ever broadening role repertoire." The fact that most women move in a sphere that can best be termed "gemeinschaft," while most men move in spheres where social relationships are more segmented, tends to restrict both the physical and the social space for women and therefore seems to account in some measure yet to be ascertained for gender differences in cognitive structures. I am referring specifically to gender differences, small as they seem to be, in mathematical performance.

The present-day division of labor by sex differs from earlier gender specialization, as when men grew wheat and women grew beans. Whereas men are expected mainly to provide the *material* resources for the family to survive, women are mainly in charge of ensuring its *social* survival. This division between men and women—where, as Judith Blake (1974) has pointed out, men in doing their jobs no longer depend on their wives, but women depend on their husbands for material support—dates from the time when the workplace became separated from the home. This separation in physical space marked the beginning of the end of gemeinschaft society.

Today, the relationships of those who go out to work are defined by and limited to precise times and precise places. This differs from relationships within the family, which remain about the same throughout the day and night. This distinction, however, does not apply equally to men and women. While the relationships outside the home are usually segmented in regard to family and co-workers in different positions, women at home are more likely to remain and to be involved in a gemeinschaft that they are in charge of maintaining.

Women, whether or not they go out to work, are expected to give priority to the family over other activity systems. Women are the pivot around which family solidarity is to be maintained and acted out, the centripetal force holding the family together (to the extent that this is possible in modern society). I have shown in Chapter 4 that a gemeinschaft is a greedy institution, one that, according to Lewis Coser (1974), absorbs all the energies of an individual and lays total claim on his or her allegiance. With Lewis Coser, I have written about the greediness of the family, about the fact that it demands total allegiance of one person, the wife/ mother, claiming priority over other possible loyalties (Coser and Coser 1974). A gemeinschaft requires complete involvement of the individual, stability of social relations, and lack of differentiation of the personality as well as of the labor performed.

Traditionally in a gemeinschaft, people's destinies are decided by fate. They generally do not choose their life-styles or their careers. A gemeinschaft also implies restriction in space. This does not mean that the physical space occupied by various persons is limited to the home or that the social space is entirely limited to the family. The true gemeinschaft of which Toennies spoke was integrated with the community, which means that family members live their lives both inside and outside of the family with relatively weak boundaries marking the separation.

The integration of the private and the public spheres in gemeinschaft society is possible in a world that is spatially restricted, and hence is restricted in the consciousness of its members. The fact that the world is round and moving has no implication for daily life in the gemeinschaft, for this fact hardly requires mental readjustment, nor is it a factor in the calculations of what is important in people's experiences. Conceptualization of space remains restricted, and abstract calculations are usually irrelevant.

A gemeinschaft, then, is a simple environment, and this is still true of the family today. Family life takes place in a relatively restricted physical space, and hence in a restricted social space as well. Like any gemeinschaft, the family is a simple relational system. Relationships are encompassed within the same social system, its members have well-defined statuses known to all, and they are known to one another. This contrasts with a complex relational system, where rules are differentiated by position, by time, and by place, and where people come from different settings. In this system, the members have different perspectives and expectations that are often incompatible and conflicting.

I have argued earlier that, where simple relationships are predominant in people's lives, they restrict the thinking process. A simple relational system does not often require individuals to become conscious of and reflect on their own roles in relation to others, since such a system hardly presents a challenge for confronting the multiple and contradictory expectations. To the extent that women are tied to the family, they miss out on such opportunities.

I am not arguing that the family, or any simple relational system for that matter, is hurtful to individuals or to the body social. On the contrary, gemeinschaft relationships help foster bonds of solidarity and give emotional support to individuals. My point here is that they are restrictive where they are the predominant type.

Family activities deal mostly with practical matters, with the nuts and bolts of everyday life. This, while important for material and emotional survival, is not conducive to creative thinking. Any one of us who has done some writing—or painting or composing—knows that one has to remove oneself from the gritty details of everyday life, from availability to other people in the gemeinschaft, in order to do serious thinking. This is so not only because thinking takes time but also because, to be creative, one has to distance oneself from preoccupations with the practicalities of the quotidian. This is why Virginia Woolf (1929) believed that a woman needs a room of her own.

The British ethologist N. K. Humphrey (1976) states: "If an ethologist had kept watch on Einstein through a pair of field glasses he might well have come to the conclusion that Einstein had a humdrum mind. But Einstein . . . displayed his genius at rare times in artificial situations; he did not use it, for he did not *need* to use it, in the common world of practical affairs" (p. 307). Humphrey makes the point that "new capacity is added only as and when it is needed" and that "subsistence technology [such as we have in gemeinschaft societies], rather than requiring intelligence, may actually become a substitute for it" (ibid.).

As I read Humphrey, he suggests that for people to develop their intelligence to its highest potential there needs to be a kind of social structure in which they are encouraged to do so. A gemeinschaft hardly provides such a structure because it tends to demand full attention to the practical affairs of the day.

Gender Differences in Cognitive Structure

In this chapter I develop the hypotheses that concerns that remain limited to the practical affairs of the present, as well as the restricted use of physical and social space, are associated with poor conceptualization of space; that and one source for the facility in mathematical thinking is to be found in the social structure.*

I begin by discussing some sex differences as they are recorded in the recent authoritative work of Eleanor Maccoby and Carol Jacklin (1974: 351). These psychologists state that there are no definitive answers to questions about psychological differences between girls and boys. In all respects except aggressiveness, the authors find the differences in psychological traits are open questions. These traits include tactile sensitivity, activity level, competitiveness, even such matters as dominance and passivity, compliance, nurturance, maternal behavior, and achievement motivation. However, according to these authors, research findings show that after the age of twelve, boys usually tend to excel over girls in visual-spatial and mathematical ability, controlling for the number of courses taken.

There is general agreement about the fact that male superiority on visual-spatial tasks is fairly consistently found in adolescence and adulthood, but not in childhood (Harris 1979; Nash

*For a discussion of evidence for and against physiological and biological explanations of cognitive differences—genetic, hormonal, neurological, cerebral—see L. J. Harris (1979); for an excellent refutation of theories of biological determinism, see Anne Fausto-Sterling (1987). See also M. A. Wittig (1976).

1979; Sherman 1967), up to a level of about .40 of a standard deviation (Maccoby and Jacklin 1974: 351–52). In regard to mathematics, Nancy Henley (1985: 108) says in her review article that "most investigators would agree that there seems to be some likelihood of a small but true difference in mathematical performance favoring boys."*

A review of the literature suggests that sex-related differences in mathematical achievement (Etaux 1983; Henley 1985; Sherman 1967) are related, at least in part, to sex-related differences in visual-spatial skills. In one school, significant gender differences in mathematical achievement were eliminated where spatial ability was controlled (Hyde et al. 1975; Sprafkin et al. 1983). However, Marcia Linn and Anne Petersen (1985), while not denying this association, question a causal relationship.

One reason for the higher scores obtained by boys in mathematical ability is what psychologists call field independence. This is the ability to restructure a problem by inhibiting a well-established response in order to take a fresh approach (Maccoby and Jacklin 1974: 104–5).† Maccoby and Jacklin found that boys and men tend to perform better than girls and women on tests relating to field independence, and that the sex difference does not emerge consistently until approximately the beginning of adolescence, paralleling the difference in spatial abilities.

In their thorough examination of theories and research on field independence, J. Kagan and H. Kogan (1970: 1334) state: "Sex differences are likely to be most pronounced between the upper elementary school grades and the last year of high school. It might be noted that these are the years when sex-role differentiation shows a pronounced increase."

Studies of field independence in people of the same genetic

* Henley (1985) quotes Janet Hyde (1981) and Joseph Rossi (1983) to the effect that, in studies such as those by Camilla Benbow and Julian Stanley (1980) and Stanley and Benbow (1982), gender differences refer mainly to the upper end of the distribution. Therefore, since the differences depend on the selection of the cutoff scores, the impression they convey is widely exaggerated.

† For an excellent explanation of the concept of field independence, see Maccoby (1963).

background from contrasting cultures have shown that those who have adopted modern life-styles have higher spatial scores than the "traditional" groups (Maccoby and Jacklin 1974: 129; Kagan and Kogan 1970). Indeed, Maccoby and Jacklin tell us that for both men and women, poorer performance on mathematical and spatial tests may stem from greater dependence, and that "where both sexes are allowed independence early in life, both sexes have good visual-spatial skills" (p. 362).*

Anne Fausto-Sterling (1987) reports that generally Eskimo outperform Temnes in tests of spatial ability, and that Eskimo boys and girls are raised permissively whereas Temne "girls are raised even more strictly than boys in this highly disciplined society" (p. 35). It turns out that, in contrast to Temne land, which is covered with vegetation, Eskimo land for hunting purposes consists of large, open, relatively featureless areas, and Eskimo language is rich in words describing geometric-spatial relationships. Not only do Eskimo show greater visual-spatial ability than Temnes, but they show no sex-related differences either. This contrasts with marked differences between Temne males and females.†

This gives me reason to hypothesize that women's shortcomings relative to those of men in regard to visual-spatial abilities are related to women's restrictions in movement in the physical field, and that their relative field dependence in thought structure is related to restrictions of, and hence dependence on, the social field. I now turn to the problem of some specific social-structural conditions that may influence analytic thinking.

In general, girls in Western society remain more dependent than boys on the habitual physical field and do not venture out into the social field the way boys do. Colin Ward (1978: 152) notes that a person "standing in a city street . . . unless in the vicinity of a girls-only school or a pop-concert," will see that "the majority of the children will be boys." In her research on children's play, Janet

---

*Julia Sherman (1982) questions the association between mathematics and independence, which other authors, including Alice Rossi (1965), have referred to.

†The methods and findings of this research, which was conducted by J. W. Berry (1966), have been reported in considerable detail by Kagan and Kogan (1970) and have also been described by Harris (1979).

Lever (1976) found that boys play outdoors far more than girls. In addition, boys' games last longer. Boys move in larger open spaces and go farther away from home during a substantial part of the day. Also, anthropological studies have shown that this is true in such faraway places as Kenya: in two different cultures, boys automatically played at a greater distance from home (Maccoby and Jacklin 1974: 196). A recent study of chasing games of second and third graders shows that the boys' games are free-floating over a large space, whereas girls have safe territories to which those who are pursued can flee (Robinson 1978).

In a study in Poland where 90 pre-adolescent children were asked what was their favorite place to be, green areas were mentioned more than twice as often by boys than by girls (25 and 11 respectively). Most boys (73 percent) mentioned "green areas," "the street," and "places of amusement," while most girls (60 percent) mentioned "home," "a friend's home," and "school" (Lynch 1977: 138; percentages constructed from figures given by Lynch).

Little is known about how the use of physical distance is initiated by adults rather than by children. It has been found that in preschool play teachers give attention to boys no matter where the boys are playing in the room, while they react to girls when they are immediately beside the teachers (Sprafkin et al. 1983). Therefore, we are not surprised to find that more often than not girls have been observed to remain close to the teacher (Maccoby and Jacklin 1974: 197), using physical space to come socially closer.

Humphrey (1976: 308) had this to say about the use of physical space:

> Some years ago I made a discovery which brought home to me dramatically the fact that . . . *a cage* is a bad place in which to keep a monkey. I was studying the recovery of vision in a rhesus monkey, Helen, from whom the visual cortex had been surgically removed. In the first four years . . . [although regaining] vision, she . . . showed no sign . . . of three-dimensional spatial vision. During all this time she had . . . been kept . . . [in] a small laboratory cage. When . . . five years after the operation, she was . . . taken for walks in the open field . . . her sight suddenly burgeoned and within a few weeks she had recovered almost perfect spatial vision; the limits of her recovery had been

imposed directly by the limited environment in which she had been living.

Humphrey suggests a direct association between movement in physical space and the development of visual-spatial ability. Let me acknowledge that I am using the example from the animal world in a manner contrary to that of the sociobiologists. I argue that if animals, whose adaptive abilities are more reliably instinctive, depend on extension of space for the development of cognitive abilities, then humans, with their notoriously weak instincts, should respond even more readily to their environment.*

There is some evidence that restricted spatial experience is related to restricted spatial conceptualization. H. A. Witkin et al. (1962) concluded from their empirical research that the limitation of children's activities and their failure to go out into the community are related to field dependence in the cognitive sense. Sherman (1967: 296) calls attention to sex-differential "learning by virtue of sex-typed activities" and notes that "boys . . . spend more time in aiming activities and games, model construction, building with blocks" and suggests that this accounts for the development of spatial skills.

Mark LaGory and John Pipkin (1981) report that, when subjects are asked to verbalize or to draw maps of urban space, performance improves with increasing socioeconomic status. The authors explain this by reference to the highly constrained activity space in the lower class. This hypothesis is confirmed in some other studies. In one by Florence Ladd (1967), in which black children were asked to draw a map of the area around their home, most children drew a very detailed picture of the area immediately surrounding home and school but depicted the nearby white housing project as a large, completely blank area on the map. On one of these maps the street dividing the neighborhoods, which in reality is of the same width as all other streets, was depicted as a boulevard nearly five times wider than any other such path. In England, B. Goodchild (1974) found that, when he asked subjects to draw maps of their environment, middle-class subjects drew more

*This is the implication of Ivan Chase's (1974; 1982) findings from his work on hierarchy in chickens.

extensive maps and displayed a more detailed knowledge of the road network than did lower-class respondents.

It seems reasonable to assume that not only class differences but also sex differences in spatial conceptualization are due to a different use of space. In a study done in Mexico City in which girls and boys were asked to draw maps of their areas, "the boys' maps contained much broader descriptions of surrounding areas [of the city]" (Lynch 1977: 155). The girls' maps did not include the surrounding areas. Of interest here is not that the girls were unacquainted with these areas, for they identified stores of the areas when presented with photographs of them. It seems that knowing about the existence of some concrete space is not sufficient for conceptualizing it. The importance of using space rather than just acquaintance with it for the conceptualization of space is indicated in this study by the fact that the boys, who were engaged in games, illustrated the surrounding areas on their city maps with sports fields, thereby showing the mental association they made between game activities and their spatial concept.

This interpretation agrees with that of B. Inhelder that the mental image in its spatial form is originally the interiorization of movements. She reported that children with richer opportunities for manipulation and visual tactile exploration have better spatial representation (Tanner and Inhelder 1958).

Changes in Adolescence

I now turn to the question of why it is that test differences between girls and boys in mathematical-analytical and spatial abilities show up at around age twelve to thirteen: What happens at that age to generate these differences? Do they arise because significant people in the environment—parents, teachers, and peers—impose their differential expectations? Why only now? And do they make themselves felt because the school curriculum has changed? What do we know about the mental orientations of boys and girls at that age and about how boys and girls become aware of their future roles?

In trying to answer these questions, I find that "support and encouragement from parents are crucial for girls in their decisions to elect or decline mathematics courses in high school" (Fox, Tobin, and Brody 1979: 314). In contrast, Sherman (1982: 437) reports that, in her study of high school seniors who had previously been tested in the ninth grade, it was hard to find much evidence of parental modeling or influence. She reports in another study, however, that one-third of the girls compared to one-tenth of the boys stated that teachers had discouraged them most in the study of mathematics. To be sure, the influences from home and school should not be ignored as at least a partial explanation of students' mathematical inclinations (cf. A. Rossi 1965).

We must also acknowledge that the curriculum has indeed changed. Before junior high school, what is called mathematics is arithmetic. Arithmetic is concrete; its problems can be solved by reference to practical problems, and evidence for their solutions can be produced in everyday practical behavior. Mathematics, in contrast, is abstract. When numbers are being replaced by a's and b's and x's and y's, the child learns to deal with the hypothetical. Generally in adolescence, thinking about the possible is being substituted for thinking about reality (Piaget, in Flavell 1963). Adolescents find out that everything they learn has a value of its own, separate from the present and from the familiar. They have to learn for the sake of learning, abstracting from present reality. It is not so much that what is to be learned is not relevant, it is *because* it is not relevant that it has to be learned. Joseph Adelson (1972: 108) states: "The most important change that we find in the transition from early to middle adolescence is the achievement of abstractness. . . . On the threshold of adolescence the child adheres to the tangible; he is most comfortable (and capable) with the concrete event, the actual person. As he matures he fights free of the concrete and its constraints and begins to reach for the abstract." This leads to the next question—namely, what are the mental orientations of adolescents?

As Kagan (1972) notes, at the start of junior high adolescents find themselves in a new social structure, one that makes more demands on their thinking. They are faced with new options. There are more organized extracurricular activities among which to choose. There is also the track system, which exists in much of the

Western world with more or less rigidity, and which forces youngsters to make decisions at age twelve to fourteen that may predetermine their careers. New courses have to be elected. Although parents may help with such choices, the youngsters themselves must think about alternatives and their consequences.

Bärbel Inhelder and Jean Piaget (1958) examine what it is at this point in the life cycle that encourages adolescents to shift from concrete to abstract and hypothetical thinking. They point out that, although still living in the present, adolescents are already oriented toward the future. "His conceptual world is full of informal theories about self and life . . . full of ideation which goes far beyond his immediate situation. . . . For him the world of future possibilities—occupational selection, marital choice, and the like—is a most important object of reflection." Adolescents will soon have to "make intellectual contact with social collectives much less concrete and immediate than family and friends: city, state, country, labor, union, church, etc." (Flavell 1963: 223).

A finding by Adelson (1972: 109) illustrates this point: "When adolescents were asked what the purpose was of a law requiring the vaccination of children, the younger interviewees said that it is to prevent children from getting sick, while older adolescents replied that it is to protect the community at large." When writing about similar phenomena, Piaget believes that such changes in orientation are intimately related to the *formal structural process* of thought. According to Inhelder and Piaget (1958), and more recently Kohlberg and Gilligan (1972), *formal operational thinking* consists in reflection about what is hypothetical. In contrast to the younger child, who thinks in terms of concrete operations, like a "sober and bookkeepish organizer of the real" (Flavell 1963: 211), adolescents are oriented in their thinking toward the possible and the hypothetical: "One manifestation of this orientation is the adolescents' tendency to explore all possibilities by subjecting the problem variables to a combinatorial analysis" (ibid. : 212).*

---

*Kagan (1972: 93) seems to agree with Piaget when he tells us: "The adolescent can deal with multiple attributes simultaneously and is not limited to a one-at-a-time analysis. This ability allows the adolescent to think about events as arrangements of multiple dimensions, and to appreciate that an experience is often dependent on events not in the immediate field."

What does this tell us about gender differences at that age? Does some gender difference in self-image or in social life develop at that time? Indeed, there is evidence that adolescent girls have less of a chance than adolescent boys to be influenced in their thinking by a broad repertoire of possibilities for the future. In the recent works I have quoted in regard to changes from the concrete to the abstract, from practical reality to the hypothetical, there is no mention of differences between boys and girls. It sounds as if "adolescents" means "boys." Or is it that at first blush it seems that boys and girls face similar choices and have to consider similar possibilities for the future? This should await the test of evidence.

It seems that, for adolescent girls, "sex-role requirements get augmented" as they get older (Nash 1979 : 285). "Most intellectual sex-related differences emerge during early adolescence, just when sex role becomes most salient to the developing male and female. Sex roles and their associated prescriptive standards may mediate cognitive performance by affecting the experiences and values put on success in a given intellectual achievement area" (p. 291).

Several studies show an association between spatial visualizations and masculinity, and a negative association with femininity (Dawson 1967; McGilligan 1971; Oetzel 1961). Nash's own research is worth noting. She found significant correlations between sex-role stereotyping of intellectual performance characteristics and spatial-visualization scores. The more masculine an adolescent boy views himself on these intellectual traits, the better his spatial performance. Similarly, the more masculine an adolescent girl views her ideal self, the better her spatial performance. Girls who preferred to be boys scored higher than girls who preferred to be girls. In fact, the scores of girls who preferred to be boys were just as high as those of boys preferring to be boys. It appears that male gender preference was associated with superior spatial performance for both sexes.

To the extent that girls do not have choice of occupation in the foreground of their consciousness with the same intensity as boys do—whether as a result of the limitations of career choices or of identification with their mothers or other adults, or in response to expectations of peers, or more generally in conformity with cultural expectations—it makes sense for girls to be concerned with what is *relevant* for the practical affairs they prepare to deal with as adults. Career choices are immensely more numerous for boys than for girls in two ways: girls see their futures as primarily determined by their sex, because they have become convinced that caring for a family will be their primary obligation. To the extent that this is so, their future is decided by fate, their focus is expected to be on the practical, and they are preparing to stay close to home. Moreover, if they should think of preparing for work outside the home, the list of possible choices is restricted because of the still prevalent sex-typing of occupations. In the professions, they have choices by and large among nursing, social work, teaching, and secretarial work, all occupations that require practical skills. Young women more often than not feel, or are made to feel, that only the very best among them—the brightest, the most energetic, the hardest working—will be able to choose among some careers that have hitherto been mainly reserved for men. It is not surprising, therefore, that one "good predictor of course-taking in mathematics for above-average-ability girls was perception of usefulness in mathematics for future career goals" (Fox, Tobin, and Brody 1979; Sherman 1982).

The formation of a girl's identity as a woman does not depend as much on her future occupation as does the formation of a boy's identity. Womanhood appears to girls to be decided by fate in ways in which manhood is not. To the extent that girls sense that they are expected to prepare to devote themselves to the family as a gemeinschaft that they will have to sustain, their biology is indeed destiny. Even though girls may have to make choices that affect their futures, they are usually convinced that having a family and caring for it is the most important thing for them to do.

It is no wonder, then, that Maccoby and Jacklin (1974: 359) found that by the time girls are a few years older, there is "the tendency for young women of college age to lack confidence in their ability to do well on a new task, and [there is] their sense that they have less control over their own fates than men do." Indeed, Nash (1979) reports that sex-related differences in self-confidence with respect to mathematics are well documented (see also Sherman 1982). Girls' self-confidence tends to decrease with age, and even when girls are achieving better than boys in mathematics they tend to rank themselves lower in ability.

In summary, it seems that self-confidence and the perception of the usefulness of mathematics are related to differences in the achievement of girls and boys. Lack of self-confidence and concern with what is practical reinforce the effect of restricted career choices for girls. If Piaget is right that ideas about a hypothetical future help bring about a change in adolescent thought structure—if thinking about the future possibilities confronting the self is related to thinking in abstract terms—then it stands to reason that adolescent girls would not be as prepared to think in abstract terms as boys are. "Logic is not isolated from life: it is no more than the expression of operational coordination essential to action" (Piaget, quoted in Flavell 1963: 223).

Interactional Patterns

In their interactional patterns as well, young adolescents begin to experience the complexity of social life, a complexity that is typical of modern society. At that time the child's network suddenly expands. Not only does it become more complex, but in one single role as student the youngster also has to deal with many more people. As Kagan (1972: 98) has pointed out, when the child between twelve and fifteen enters junior high or high school, an important change in social behaviors takes place:

> Unlike the elementary school, the junior high and high school contain many more individuals who hold different beliefs. The beliefs concern drugs, sex, authority, the value of study, and attitudes toward parents. Each ideological position has many advocates. The sources of these new views cannot easily be discredited and the adolescent must deal with the dissonance.

In order to discuss the differential opportunities for dealing with this dissonance, it is useful to introduce once again the concept of role-set (Merton 1968d: 422–40), which, it will be remembered, refers to the various role partners a person has and the

ensuing incompatibilities and conflicts among them in their expectations. I want to add that the frequency of incompatibilities
and conflicts in the role-set is directly related to its social heterogeneity or, as I have called it in this book, its complexity. I have
argued that in a simple role-set, even if some role partners are differently situated than others (e.g., because of authority relations),
there are characteristically few differences in outlook and expectations among them, and they do not reveal much that is new or
unexpected.

Already before junior high, but especially at that time, girls
have less complex role-sets than boys. This means that girls have
less opportunity than boys do to deal with the dissonance of
which Kagan speaks. As we have seen in Chapter 4, complex role-
sets require participants to take account of various perspectives, to
exercise judgment, to negotiate, and to compromise. This requires an effort, first to differentiate among the various perspectives and to articulate the possible conflicts, then to reconcile
them or to make choices. In this way one learns to articulate one's
own role in relation to the multiple role partners.

In junior high school, role-sets suddenly become more complex. No longer does the child have to deal with only one teacher,
the principal, and other children of the same age. Now there are
different teachers for every subject, of different status and orientations, and with different expectations. Moreover, in the various
classrooms a child visits during the course of a day, there are different students each time, often of different ages, rather than the
same familiar group of peers. The youngsters thus learn about
more perspectives; they understand better that the world is larger
than their own little worlds at home and at the old school. We
have heard Kagan say that children have to learn to deal with all
these differences—that is, with the incompatibilities and contradictions in expectations of their many and various new as well as
old role partners.

In regard to this kind of role-set complexity, there is little difference between boys and girls. But not all their time is spent in
formal learning in different classrooms. They also interact with
one another at lunch, in the corridors and on staircases on the way

from one classroom to another, and before and after school, and they spend much of their waking time at play and games. It is in those situations that girls interact differently from boys.

It will be remembered that boys play outdoors more often than girls do, and I used this example to show that boys use physical space more extensively. There are other differences. Outdoor games involve more children than indoor games, but even girls' outdoor games involve fewer people than do boys' outdoor games. The contest plays of girls, such as hopscotch or jacks, can be played with as few as two people, whereas team games, which are what boys usually play, need a larger number of players.

In general, girls move in dyads or triads whereas boys spend their time with a larger group of peers. Lever (1976) finds that girls are uncomfortable in groups of four or more. Even earlier, as Maccoby and Jacklin (1974: 207) note, at around age seven "Girls are focusing their play in intensive relations with one or two 'best friends,'" while boys play in larger groups.

Moreover, not only are there more role partners in the play of boys, but there is also more diversity among them, for the boys' play partners are usually more heterogeneous agewise. Also, as Lever notes, boys' games last longer than girls' games, both at school during recess and outside of school. Not only, then, are their role-sets more complex but, in addition, boys are more engaged with their game partners. And, regardless of the number and nature of the participants, boys' games require a complex process of interaction in their very rule systems. Brian Sutton-Smith (1979: 251) made observations that are similar to those of Lever about sex differences in game playing; he concludes that "despite . . . the great changes that have taken place in the play of girls during the last seventy years, the dominant impression is of girls pursuing traditional female ways." He quotes from the research of L. Hughes (1977) in a small rural town:

> Boys reported high levels of participation in organized youth and sports groups . . . in formal team sports . . . and in fishing and hunting. In contrast, girls did more homework and chores in the home, and cared for brothers and sisters. . . . No strong patterns of game involvement or participation in organized

community activities emerged for the girls. . . . Girls' repertoires of games and lore were also very weak in comparison to boys' repertoires. . . . Girls' emphasis on small group activities, and more specifically the quality of their social relationships with a small group of friends, contrasted sharply with boys' strong emphasis on team sports and other activities involving physical skill and competition as their basis of interaction with peers. (Sutton-Smith 1979: 250–51)

In a study by Margaret Hennig and Anne Jardin (1977), we find full realization of the complexities of team play and the idea that girls are traditionally deprived of this learning opportunity. Thomas Boslooper and Marcia Hayes (1979), as quoted by Sutton-Smith (1979), point out that girls more often play games of chance, whereas boys are more often engaged in games of strategy.

Team games are games in the sociological sense of the term, as distinct from contests, for example. I refer to the fact that, in games, the participants modify one another's behavior. I distinguish between *play* (skating, skiing, bicycle riding), *contests* (bicycle racing, hopscotch, jacks, jumprope), and *games* (baseball, football, chess). Only the latter type are games in the restricted sociological definition. Although in contests psychological and sociological processes may influence the participants, as in the bowling game—or bowling contest, in sociological terms—described by Whyte (1943), such influential factors are extrinsic to the rules of the game. By stating that cognitive complexity, by which they mean "the utilization of several dimensions of cognition," is obtained by taking the point of view of other persons, Siegfried Streufert and Susan Streufert (1978: 91) echo what G. H. Mead (1946: 153–54) has to say about the game:

> The fundamental difference between the game and play is that in the game the child must have [in mind] the attitudes of all the other players involved in that game. The attitudes of the other players which the participant assumes organize into a sort of unit. . . . This unit becomes the *generalized other* as it enters—as an organized process and social activity—into the experience of any one of the individual members of it.

And Humphrey (1976: 309) explains the interaction process of the chess game: "Given that each move in the game may call forth several alternative responses from the other player, [the] forward planning [of the gamesman] will take the form of a decision tree, having its root in the current situation and growing branches. . . . [The branches correspond] to the moves that are considered in looking at different possibilities" from the vantage point of the current situation; "It asks for a level of intelligence which is, I submit, unparalleled in any other sphere of living."

As I read Mead and Humphrey, their models of a game do not include contests such as hopscotch and jacks. If, however, one includes such contest play in the class of games, as Lever does in her study, it turns out that 65 percent of the boys' activities were what she calls "formal games" as compared to only 35 percent of the girls' activities. Had Lever used my distinction, restricting the category of games to those that involve mutually modifying interaction, the difference would have been even greater, since hopscotch, jacks, and jumprope would have been eliminated in her calculations of the girls' so-called games.

The importance of games for conceptual organization is described by the French social scientist Georges Mesmin (1973: 34–35): "The game offers an affirmation of the self and a confrontation with others. It is also a means of organizing space intellectually. . . . When the time comes [for junior high], the child will make the step from the practical and concrete—which is based on action—to conceptual thinking—which is subject to *universal* rules" (my translation; emphasis added).

From her own findings and from the accumulated evidence, as well as from Mead's definition of games, Lever astutely concludes that "boys [more often] develop the ability to take the role of the *generalized other* whereas girls are more likely to develop empathy, to take the role of the *particular other*" (p. 485). Lever could have added, using Parsons's typology, that this means that girls are getting prepared for *particularistic* relationships, which are more typical of gemeinschaft as I showed in Chapter 4. These contrast with *universalistic* relationships, which are typical of modern segmented society.

The difference refers to the distinction, it will be remembered, that Talcott Parsons (1951: 61–63) makes between particularism and universalism. In particularistic relationships, people remain tied to concrete individuals. They know one another's concrete problems and remain focused on them, like the girls interviewed by Lever who said that they learned to know their friend "and her moods so well that through non-verbal cues alone, a girl understands whether her playmate is hurt, sad, happy, bored and so on" (p. 484).* In particularistic relationships, one does not have to make much effort to put oneself imaginatively in the position of the other person, for the intimacy is such that one *knows* the other person's feelings. In this case, feelings do not have to be articulated, which means that they do not have to be intellectualized.

In contrast, a universalistic relationship is one in which the partners are not considered unique: one salesperson—*as a salesperson*, that is—can substitute for another, and so can an employer—*as an employer*. In G. H. Mead's (1946: 153–54) words, it is "in abstract thought [that] the individual takes the attitude of the generalized other toward himself, without reference to its expression in any particular individual."

Social complexity, then, seems to be related to the use and development of cognitive skills. Humphrey tells a charming story about how he made this discovery. It will be remembered that his own rhesus monkey, Helen, recovered her three-dimensional spatial vision after he took her out of the cage for walks in the open field. Humphrey then compares his cage with a larger one containing some eight or nine monkeys, with plenty of room to move about but without any objects to manipulate. This gave him cause for worry. He continues:

> And then one day I saw a half-weaned infant pestering its mother, two adolescents engaged in a mock battle, an old male grooming a female whilst another female tried to sidle up to him, and I suddenly saw the scene with new eyes: forget about the absence of *objects*, these monkeys had *each other* to manipulate and to explore. There could be no risk of their dying an

---

*From their research entitled "Sex Differences in the Self-Concept in Adolescence," Florence Rosenberg and Roberta Simmons (1975: 159) conclude that, though "excessive concern with interpersonal relations and excessive sensitivity to others may be admirable traits in some circumstances . . . , both achievement and self-fulfillment among girls may be seriously impeded by overconcern with others, a concern traditionally associated with the female stereotype."

intellectual death when the social environment provided such
obvious opportunity for participating in a running dialectical
debate. (p. 308)

I note that Humphrey stresses the importance of diversity in social relations for the development of intelligence. This gives me
the opportunity to say a few more words about complexity in social relationships.

Complexity of Role-Sets

As I have suggested throughout this work, a complex role-set
forces its members to negotiate and to make compromises between different, often incompatible or even contradictory expectations and points of view. It is interesting to note that Lever
found that "boys could resolve their disputes more effectively
[than girls did]. They were seen quarreling all the time, but not
once was a game terminated because of a quarrel [which is what
happened in girls' games]. . . . In the gravest debates, the final
word was always to repeat the play. . . . [The] boys seemed to enjoy the legal debates every bit as much as the game itself" (p. 482).
The only time Piaget (1948: 69) hints at gender differences is
when he briefly states: "We didn't succeed in finding a single collective game played by girls in which there were as many rules
and, above all, as fine and consistent an organization and codifi-
cation of these rules as in the game of marbles [which was played
by boys]."

It is in a complex social setting with its incompatibilities that
there evolves a system of deliberately articulated rules that serve to
guide interaction. It is in terms of rules that choices can be made,
and such rules, as we have learned from Lewis Coser (1956), are
frequently being established as a result of conflict. Kohlberg and
Gilligan (1972: 179) state that "experimental intervention can to
some extent accelerate cognitive development if it is based on
providing experiences of *cognitive conflict* which stimulate the
child to reorganize or rethink his patterns of cognitive ordering"
(emphasis added).

Conflicts in role relationships force people to distance themselves both socially and emotionally and to reflect about their own stance. As John Dewey (1930: 300) has noted, conflict is the sine qua non of reflection and ingenuity.

Social conflicts are endemic in complex role-sets. In the face of conflicting expectations, one is forced to reflect and to articulate one's role. (Spatial distance helps, of course, not only for social and emotional distance, but also because it permits one to withdraw from observability [R. Coser 1961] and in this way to manipulate one's relationships. When one's behavior cannot be observed directly by all role partners—and in this respect social life differs from games—manipulation becomes easier.) This accounts for the findings of Melvin Kohn (1969a) about the correlation between environmental complexity and intellectual flexibility. On the basis of the latest large-scale research efforts of Kohn and his associates (1983), Carmi Schooler (1984) shows that substantive complexity of the environment correlates with cognitive orientation. The 1983 research team also confirmed earlier findings about the effect of social complexity on intellectual flexibility, and it revealed that this holds for women as it does for men.

A group of psychologists who call themselves the Genevans have established this relation between conflict and cognitive progress in a large body of experimental research (see, e.g., Doise and Mugny 1979). They state that a central condition for cognitive progress to occur through social interaction is that "the interaction entail opposition of divergent cognitive responses" (Mugny, DePaolis, and Carugati 1984: 143). They also state that one important source of such conflict is an encounter between participants "occupying positions or points of view (particularly spatial) that generate divergent responses" (ibid.).

To resolve conflicts between divergent responses, one has to be able to create distance, and this is more readily done in segmented relationships because in simple role-sets—such as those of the family—a woman is involved with her whole personality. To be in a position of mentally detaching oneself from the social field of interaction is as important for abstract thinking as is physical distance for spatial conceptualization.

A story told by Hennig and Jardin (1977) and quoted by

Sutton-Smith (1979: 253) is to the point here. A junior bank officer recalls her twelve-year-old brother complaining every Saturday about two of the boys he played football with. She finally asked him, "If you don't like them, why do you play with them?" The brother's response was, "You've got to be crazy. We need eleven for the team." The woman says now, "I thought about it a lot and I simply couldn't understand it. I knew that if I felt like that about another girl, there was no way I would have played with her." Sutton-Smith comments that it throws light on the fact that women in organizations often cannot understand why their office tolerates an incompetent male worker: "They could not realize that typical male organizations are relatively impersonal and involve a weighing of pros and cons and a balancing of skills in order to get a result. The close relationships that women cherish and that are part of the prototypical nuclear family are not the basic kind of relationships on which work organizations are based" (p. 253).

The story implies that women are engaged in less segmented relationships and that this pattern is consistent ever since childhood. Nancy Chodorow (1978) argues that the little girl remains tied to the mother in an affectively diffuse relationship for a much longer time than the little boy, who turns to his father and learns with his help to turn his energies outward from the home. This contention is consistent with my observations in public places, of little boys usually running and roaming while little girls are more likely to stay put—on the lap or in an embrace or in conversation with their mother. Sutton-Smith believes that much of girls' play models on the mother-child situation and implies that, although "considerable sensitivity to other persons is [probably] being developed through this activity" (p. 246), it also prepares girls for "the woman's sensitivity to the dominant husband" (p. 247).

Of course, neither these authors nor I believe that what happens in early childhood or in adolescence predetermines adult patterns in irreversible fashion. As I have noted in the previous chapter, adult patterns can be explained in terms of earlier stages of development only when there is continuity of experiences all through the life cycle. Where discontinuities occur—and I have argued that college life is an important occasion for this—the pattern might well be reversed, as it has been for a minority of women over the decades. Nevertheless, for many women even today the cultural pattern is being maintained.

The Use of Space Throughout the Life Cycle

With the cultural mandate for women to take care of home and family comes the expectation that they stay close to home as well (though perhaps not to the extent described by the immigrant women quoted at the beginning of this chapter). My Israeli colleague Rivka Bar-Yosef (1974; oral communication) has reported that married Israeli soldiers at the front have stated that they find it reassuring that their wives are at home while they themselves do the fighting. Recall that we also learned from research done in Poland that young boys usually mention the outdoors as their favorite places to be, in contrast to the girls, who tend to mention their home or a friend's home (Lynch 1977). Thus we understand that the girls indeed seem to get prepared for their future careers in homemaking. In another study, girls and boys were asked to describe a typical day in their life as an adult. Even the girls initially indicating a career goal other than homemaking described their anticipated typical day as spent being a wife or mother rather than at a job outside the home (Iglitzin 1972).

To keep girls and women close to home we do not have to engage in brutal coercion, as did the Chinese of yesteryear with their footbinding practices. There, "the constraint on female movement was one of the benefits of footbinding appreciatively noted by Confucian patriarchs. 'Why must the foot be bound? To prevent barbarous running around'" (Stacey 1983: 41).

Elsewhere I have written (1975b) that there is an unspoken rule against women traveling on their own, especially if they are of childbearing age. For example, we learn that in the past some nurses who traveled often "were considered a recurrent problem" and that this was "diagnosed" by one physician as a "strange pathological malady—itching foot" (Pape 1964: 338). Although this example may seem to be out of the ordinary, it highlights the disapproval of a woman on the road. Unlike the man who inspires more confidence if he cultivates the appearance of a "family man," a woman who gives the appearance of a "family woman" (note the strange sound of the expression) would evoke suspicion if she had an occupation demanding travel on foreign territory. In general, it is when she does not appear to be a "family woman" that she is more readily accepted in her occupational role. Until recently, preference for a youthful appearance in a flight attendant, though in part dictated by sex appeal, was at least equally due to the transitory status of the young woman, one that is acceptable before but not during motherhood. A mother belongs at home, not on the road or in the air.

As physical space remains restricted, so does social space. This means that women in general have less opportunity than men do to operate in a complex role-set. For example, not only do fewer women belong to voluntary associations (Babchuck and Booth 1969; Booth 1972), but the associations they belong to are much smaller in size (McPherson and Smith-Lovin 1982). This has important consequences not only in regard to restriction of vision and of thinking processes, as I have noted, but in regard to career and job opportunities as well. Also, women belong to different types of associations (ibid.). They are more often affiliated with community organizations, whereas men are more often affiliated with national organizations. Another difference is that women often belong to the women's auxiliaries of men's organizations (ibid.). There they meet other women more or less similarly situated, which means that their role partners do not, as the Genevans state, occupy different positions or hold much different points of view. In business organizations, the size ratio of men's associations to women's is four to one. That is, even businesswomen do not have as many or as important role partners as men have. Further, men's labor unions are more than twice as large as women's: "Taken together with the finding that there are nearly six times as many male union members to begin with, this fact assures male domination in the union sector of the voluntary system" (ibid.: 889). Male dominance is assured, but so is female isolation from those who dominate.

Differences in affiliation are related to gender differences in the life cycle. When examining affiliation by age, Miller McPherson and Lynn Smith-Lovin (1982) show that, for men, affiliation peaks steeply around age 55—that is, when they are at the height of their careers. At that time, women's affiliations, which show no steep peak, decrease significantly. This is the time when there are no more children in the home—that is, when the career of mother-hood has ended and when, probably for this reason, women have fewer ties to the outside community. The authors conclude that "family events [are] important in determining women's associa-tional behavior in the voluntary sector" (p. 893), whereas for men, career cycle is more important.

Further evidence that women's affiliations are related to the gemeinschaft nature of their roles comes from the fact that "when men and women are in school or keeping house, they belong to organizations very similar in size," and "when women are in the labor force full-time they tend to belong to much larger organiza-tions than [do] housewives" (McPherson and Smith-Lovin 1982: 890). It seems that "size differences in men's and women's organi-zations are related to differing positions held in the economic sec-tor" (ibid.). The vicious cycle is clear: women's organizations are less important and smaller because of their restricted career and job opportunities, a consequence of their family roles, as we have seen in the previous chapter. In turn, the nature of their jobs, with their lack of complex role-sets, further maintains women in their place.

It has not been my purpose to explore in this chapter the ex-tent to which the gender-differential patterns I have outlined are the result of direct discrimination. Here I have only tried to add some understanding to the riddle of sex differences in conceptual thinking by relating the development of abstract thought to two points: first, to the choices facing adolescents in regard to hypo-thetical and possible careers; and, second, to the differential use of physical and social space by girls and boys and by women and men. Regarding the first point, girls are limited in their oppor-tunities for hypothetical planning for the future, both because of women's cultural mandate and because of the sex-typing of occu-pations. Girls' minds are kept fixated on practical, concrete affairs and are kept from developing their full reflective capabilities. Re-garding the second point, anticipation of a career as housewife and homemaker also keeps girls closer to home all through life. Girls and women by and large do not move as far away from home as boys do, nor do they have role-sets as complex as those of boys and men. My friends in network theory would argue, and I agree with them, that smaller networks offer fewer opportunities for jobs and careers (Granovetter 1974). But this is not what I am talking about here. The reason I talk about role-sets rather than networks is because I want to emphasize the structural differences and incompatibilities among role partners. Simpler role-sets do not merely offer fewer opportunities for careers and jobs; they do not provide the conflicting expectations, to paraphrase Dewey (1930: 300), that stir us to observation and memory, that instigate us to invention, that shock us out of sheep-like passivity.

Summary and Conclusions

To the extent that women and girls are encouraged to focus primarily on the practicalities of everyday life, they will face limited opportunities to think hypothetically and to venture out both physically and socially. This means that, to the extent they are expected to devote themselves to a gemeinschaft, with daily concerns for the family, they will stay closer to home and will encourage their daughters to do the same.* All through childhood and adolescence, girls do not use space as extensively as boys do, nor do they partake of complex social relations in game activities.

The use of physical space would seem to be associated with its conceptualization,† and insofar as this is related to the ability to

*Compare Patricia Gurin's (1987: 174) comments: "Some statuses facilitate the acquisition of new statuses while others retard it. For example, the status of paid worker tends to lead to membership in a professional organization or union. Some work statuses within a national or multinational company lead not only to additional statuses but also to cosmopolitan experiences and exposure to widely divergent perspectives. In contrast, the status of mother has historically precluded many statuses; even when it did lead to additional statuses, they were nearly always located in the local environment."

†After this book was substantively written, Maryann Baenninger and Nora Newcombe's (1989) article on spatial test performance came to my attention. From this paper we learn that, in general, for both sexes, spatial activity appears to be related to spatial ability; that there is a gender difference

think at a high level of abstraction, girls are hampered in their developing mathematical abilities.

Restricted use of physical space is associated with restricted use of social space, as residential segregation, for example, amply testifies. More generally, a change in place is likely to imply a change in social environment and an extension of social relations.

That physical distancing is related to mental distancing is implied in the psychological concept of field independence and its antonym, field dependence. This, psychologists claim, is associated with a lack of mathematical ability. It means that restriction in the use of space keeps people dependent on the habitual field, literally speaking.

This raises the question of the relation of abstract thinking to the structure of social relationships. I have tried to show that a complex relational system, in contrast to a simple one, offers opportunities for reflection, for social and psychological distance, and hence for developing abstract thought.

As of the 1980's, the behaviors I have been talking about in regard to women's primary orientation toward work and family roles are in the process of change. From the accumulated evidence about changes during the past two decades, we know that women have increased their participation in the occupational world. We learn from the census that from 1972 to 1979, while the proportion of women in medicine increased by less than one percentage point (10.1 to 10.7), it doubled in pharmacy (from 12.4 to 24.4) and more than doubled in dentistry (2.0 to 4.5) and in printing press operation (4.8 to 11.5), to name only a few traditionally male occupations. The presence of women more than tripled in engineering (.8 to 2.9), including electrical and electronic engineering (7.0 to 22.0) and industrial engineering (2.4 to 7.3), and in law (3.8 to 12.4), and almost quadrupled in radio and television mechanics (.8 to 3.1) (Kaplan and Van Valey 1980). By 1980, 13.4 percent of physicians were women, and 13.8 percent of lawyers, 17.1 percent of

---

in both spatial ability and spatial activity; that increases in spatial experience improve spatial ability; and that spatial ability test performance can be improved by training for both sexes, and improvement does not appear different for males and females.

judges (up from 6.1 in 1970), and 4.6 percent of engineers. Most important for the subject matter of this chapter, during the 1970's women increased their participation in the natural sciences from 13.6 to 19.9 percent, and in mathematical and computer sciences by almost 10 percent, from 16.7 to 26.1 percent; among teachers in post-secondary mathematics and computer sciences, women's participation increased from 29.3 to 32.3 percent (*Statistical Abstracts* 1985, 105th ed., U.S. Department of Commerce, Bureau of the Census, p. 400).

It therefore seems fair to assume that girls today have more choices and that women have gradually increased their participation in large organizations and have extended their movements in social space generally. Also, girls have to some extent, however small, begun to play more complex games. In short, girls and women today have more complex role-sets, tend to be less focused on gemeinschaft, and are less limited in their concern with the practicalities of everyday life than they were a decade or two ago.

Are there any changes in cognitive structure? A longitudinal study conducted jointly by Harold Stevenson of the University of Michigan and Richard Newman of the State University of New York at Stony Brook, begun in the mid-1970's, shows that some change can be recorded: in elementary school, girls no longer equal boys in arithmetic performance, they excel over boys. And among the oldest children in the study, who are in tenth grade, there are no longer any gender differences in mathematical abilities (Stevenson and Newman 1985). The change so far is important, even though we do not yet know whether the trend of boys' superiority in mathematics will get reestablished after age fifteen.

I now turn to a statement by the famous scientist Peter Medawar (1976: 501), which I want to make my own: "Anybody who professes to discern a moralizing flavor in what I have been writing is perfectly right: it is exactly what I intend. I think we shall have to get used to the idea that moral judgments should intrude into the execution and application of science at every level." In this spirit I must mention that, as I have been reflecting on women's use of space, I remembered hearing my father say: "If Amelia

Earhart can fly across the Atlantic, women can do anything!" By now women have been launched into space. We can foresee the time when it will no longer be necessary to sing with Harry Chapin that "The girls were told to reach the shelves / While the boys were reaching stars."

Epilogue

What I have been saying in this book in dispraise of gemeinschaft may surprise some of my friends. My moral and political stance, like that of many academics, is on the political left. Yet, by and large this Left has argued that time and again the malaise, the anomie, the sense of mutual estrangement that characterize our age are due to the lack of community. As Suzanne Keller (1988) put it in her presidential address to the Eastern Sociological Society: "Our age is still in search of community." Or, as Kai Erikson (1986) said in his presidential address to the American Sociological Association: "If alienation is a state of being, it does not reside in the workplace alone but in the whole of one's existence" in modern society.

I have little quarrel with these statements in regard to their general meaning. I recognize, like many do, the multiple symptoms of sickness in an acquisitive society: the rising rates of suicide, divorce, and homicide, the increasing poverty, and the widening gap between the rich and the poor. Where I differ from many of my colleagues is not the recognition of malaise and anomie in modern society. My quarrel is with their suggested remedies.

Both anomie and individual creativity have their source in modernity, and the problem at hand is to try to overcome the one and foster the other. Poverty and powerlessness—the main sources of alienation, it seems to me—offer a bad foundation for the development of individual autonomy, intellectual flexibility, and creativity. If I be permitted some social science lingo (once more), the structure of social relations is the intervening variable between conditions of poverty and powerlessness, on the one hand, and the inability of whole sectors of the society to enlarge their horizon and their aspirations, on the other.

I believe that it is stultifying for the individual to be submerged in poverty and powerlessness—conditions that encourage unidimensional relationships—be it in their work, in a gemeinschaft society, in a cult, or oftentimes in the family. There is no need to elaborate here on the dehumanizing effects of routinized work, but I want to repeat what I said about the nature of a gemeinschaft society: it does not empower; it *disempowers* because it deprives individuals of that richness of perspective that comes from a multiplicity of relationships. Such multiplicity is largely denied to some social strata, like the lower class—and this includes race where it is associated with poverty—and still to a large extent to women, at least to those women who, for reasons of social structure and cultural pressure, are relegated to home and household.

Nobody can argue that we do not need more of a sense of community; even those who are little inclined to do what it takes talk of the need of a kinder and gentler society. We would all like to see a strengthening of a sense of loyalty among our citizens, a better sense of mutual obligation between friends, between spouses, and between parents and children. The problem is how to develop mechanisms and policies that make it possible to strengthen such ties without their becoming so strong as to hamper role segmentation—that is, the participation of individuals in multiple and diverse relationships that benefit both the body social and themselves as creative, autonomous individuals.

The last two chapters in this book should leave no doubt about my feminist stance. I do not advocate that women become as detached from their fellow beings as many men are, especially those who are on the fast tracks of their careers. Since traditionally women have been relegated to the gemeinschaft of the family, their learned dispositions for personal relatedness can be usefully integrated in a segmented structure of relationships. While I believe that women are every inch as capable as men are to advance their own interests for the sake of individual achievement by distancing themselves from their strong ties, I hope that they will not give up their capacity to nurture and their willingness to care for others. Role segmentation does not mean that there should be no bonding. It only means that modern society provides the opportunity for both attachment and detachment for the benefit of participation in pluralistic relationships. In a segmented society, men *and* women can do both. Men can come closer and women can gain some distance, so that both men and women can engage in autonomous individualized behavior—with the help, no doubt, of better conditions for fostering mutual support.

It would be foolish to claim that the availability of structural opportunities for individuation in itself is a guarantee for healthy rational discourse. Not all who are well placed to do so will partake of such opportunities. Nevertheless, more people will derive benefit from those opportunities than if such opportunities were not available. Such availability is a necessary though not sufficient condition for individual and collective rationality.

Like everyone else, I am not in a position to offer a panacea for the ills our society makes us endure. And I would distrust anyone who makes such a claim. I believe only that these ills cannot be alleviated by advocating collective bliss at the price of personal freedom and individual autonomy. What we need is a society where, to use an idea dear to Jürgen Habermas, all citizens have an occasion to participate in a rational discourse between many segments of the population, in a give-and-take imbued with sentiments that are tempered by criss-crossing relationships. Such a pluralistic give-and-take can be made into the foundation of a community of equal participants. I hope that such a society could generate both the multiplicity of perspectives and the mutual support it takes for the enlargement of our aspirations, which are needed for efficacious individualism.

Reference Matter

WORKS CITED

Adelson, Joseph
  1972 "The Political Imagination of the Young Adolescent." In Kagan and Coles, eds., 1972: 106–43.
Aiken, Michael, and Jerald Hage
  1966 "Organizational Alienation: A Comparative Analysis." *ASR* 31: 497–507.
Allardt, Erik
  1975 "Samhallsstruktur." In Melvin Seeman, "Alienation Studies." *Annual Review of Sociology*: 91–123.
Angell, Robert Cooley
  1956 *The Two Major Works of Charles H. Cooley.* Glencoe, Ill.: Free Press.
Babchuck, Nicholas, and Alan Booth
  1969 "Voluntary Associations." *ASR* 34: 31–45.
Baenninger, Maryann, and Nora Newcombe
  1989 "The Role of Experience in Spatial Performance: A Meta-Analysis." *Sex Roles* 20: 327–44.
Bailyn, Lotte
  1984 "Issues of Work and Family in Organizations: Responding to Social Diversity." In Michael B. Arthur, Lotte Bailyn, Daniel J. Levinson, and Herbert A. Shepard, *Working with Careers.* New York: Center for Research in Career Development, Columbia University.
Bar-Yosef, Rivka
  1974 Paper presented at the Annual Meeting of the Society for the Study of Social Problems, Montreal.
Bateson, P. P. G., and R. A. Hinde, eds.
  1976 *Growing Points in Ethology.* Cambridge, Eng.: Cambridge University Press.
Baum, Charlotte, Paula Hyman, and Sonya Michel
  1977 *The Jewish Woman in America.* New York: Plume Books.

Benbow, Camilla P., and Julian C. Stanley
1980 "Sex Difference in Mathematical Ability: Fact or Artifact?" *Science* 210: 1262–64.

Berger, Peter L., Brigitte Berger, and Hansfried Kellner
1973 *The Homeless Mind.* New York: Random House.

Bernstein, Basil
1971 *Class, Codes, and Control.* Vol. 1. London: Routledge & Kegan Paul.

Berry, J. W.
1966 "Temne and Eskimo Perceptual Skills." *International Journal of Psychology* 1: 207–29.

Blake, Judith
1974 "Changing Status of Women in Developed Countries." *Scientific American* 231: 24, 136–47.

Blau, Judith R.
1980 "Paradoxical Consequences of Excesses in Structural Complexity: A Study of a State Children's Psychiatric Hospital." *Sociology of Health and Illness* 2: 227–92.

Blau, Judith R., and Richard D. Alba
1982 "Empowering Nets of Participation." *Administrative Science Quarterly* 27: 363–79.

Blau, Peter M.
1964 *Exchange and Power in Social Life.* New York: Wiley.
1977 *Inequality and Heterogeneity: A Primitive Theory of Social Structure.* New York: Free Press.

Blauner, Robert
1964 *Alienation and Freedom: The Factory Worker and His Industry.* Chicago: University of Chicago Press.

Boldt, Edward D.
1978 "Structural Tightness, Autonomy, and Observability: An Analysis of Hutterite Conformity and Orderliness." *Canadian Journal of Sociology* 3: 349–63.

Booth, Alan
1972 "Sex and Social Participation." *ASR* 37: 183–89.

Bosk, Charles L.
1979 *Forgive and Remember: Managing Medical Failure.* Chicago: University of Chicago Press.

Boslooper, Thomas, and Marcia Hayes
1979 *The Femininity Game.* New York: Stein & Day.

Bourdieu, Pierre
1980 "Le Capital Social." *Actes de la recherche en sciences sociales* 31: 2–3.

Bourguière, André
1980 "Un nom pour soi: Le choix du nom de baptême en France sous l'Ancien Régime (XVIe–XVIIIe siècles)." *L'Homme* 20: 25–42.

Bronfenbrenner, Urie
1979 *The Ecology of Human Development: Experiments by Nature and Design*. Cambridge, Mass.: Harvard University Press.
Bruner, Jerome S.
1966 "On Cognitive Growth, II." In Bruner et al., eds., 1966: 30–67.
Bruner, Jerome S., et al., eds.
1966 *Studies in Cognitive Growth*. New York: Wiley
Burns, Tom
1953 "Friends, Enemies, and Polite Fiction." *ASR* 18: 654–62.
Chase, Ivan D.
1974 "Models of Hierarchy Formation in Animal Societies." *Behavioral Science* 19: 374–82.
1982 "Behavioral Sequences During Dominance Hierarchy in Chickens." *Science* 216: 439–40.
Chevallier, Gabriel
1963 *Clochemerle-Les-Bains*. New York: Simon and Schuster.
Chodorow, Nancy
1978 *The Reproduction of Mothering: Psychoanalysis and the Sociology of Gender*. Berkeley: University of California Press.
Cohen, Y. A.
1971 "The Shaping of Men's Minds: Adaptations to Imperatives of Culture," in M. L. Wax, S. Diamond, and F. O. Gearing, eds., *Anthropological Perspectives on Education*. New York: Basic Books.
Collins, Randall
1988 *Durkheimian Sociology: Cultural Studies*. Cambridge, Eng.: Cambridge University Press.
Coser, Lewis A.
1956 *The Functions of Social Conflict*. Glencoe, Ill.: Free Press.
1967 "Some Functions of Deviant Behavior and Normative Flexibility." In *Continuities in the Study of Social Conflict*. New York: Free Press, 111–33.
1974 *Greedy Institutions*. New York: Free Press.
Coser, Lewis A., ed.
1975 *The Idea of Social Structure: Papers in Honor of Robert K. Merton*. New York: Harcourt Brace Jovanovich.
Coser, Rose Laub
1958 "Authority and Decision-Making in a Hospital: A Comparative Analysis." *ASR* 23: 56–63.
1960 "Laughter Among Colleagues: A Study of the Social Functions of Humor Among the Staff of a Mental Hospital." *Psychiatry* 23: 81–95.
1961 "Insulation from Observability and Types of Social Conformity." *ASR* 26: 28–39.

1963 "Alienation and the Social Structure: A Case Analysis of a Hospital." In Eliot Freidson, ed., *The Hospital in Modern Society*. New York: Free Press, 231–65.

1966 "Role Distance, Sociological Ambivalence and Transitional Status Systems." *American Journal of Sociology* 62: 173–87.

1975a "The Complexity of Roles as a Seedbed of Individual Autonomy." In L. Coser, ed., 1975: 237–63.

1975b "Stay Home, Little Sheba: On Placement, Displacement and Social Change." *Social Problems* 22: 470–80.

1979 *Training in Ambiguity: Learning Through Doing in a Mental Hospital*. New York: Free Press.

1984 "The Greedy Nature of Gemeinschaft." In Powell and Robbins, eds., 1984: 221–39.

1986 "Cognitive Structure and the Use of Social Space." *Sociological Forum* 1: 1–26.

Coser, Rose Laub, ed.

1969 *Life Cycle and Achievement in America*. New York: Harper Torch Books.

1974 *The Family, Its Structures and Functions*. With an Introduction. New York: St. Martin's.

Coser, Rose Laub, and Lewis A. Coser

1974 "The Housewife and Her Greedy Family." In L. Coser 1974: 89–100.

1979 "Jonestown as Perverse Utopia." *Dissent* 26: 158–63.

Coser, Rose Laub, and Gerald Rokoff

1971 "Women in the Occupational World." *Social Problems* 18: 535–54.

Covello, Leonard

1967 *The Social Background of the Italo-American School Child*. Leiden: Brill.

Crosby, Faye J., ed.

1987 *Spouse, Parent, Worker: On Gender and Multiple Roles*. New Haven, Conn.: Yale University Press.

Davis, Fred, and Virginia L. Oleson

1963 "Initiation into a Woman's Profession: Identity Problems in the Status Transition of Co-ed to Student Nurse." *Sociometry* 26: 89–101.

1965 "The Career Outlook of Professionally Educated Women." *Psychiatry* 28: 334–45.

Davis, Kingsley

1949 *Human Society*. New York: Macmillan.

Dawson, J. L. M.

1967 "Cultural and Physiological Influence Upon Spatial-Perceptual Processes in West Africa." *International Journal of Psychology* 28: 115–28, 171–85.

Dewey, John
1930 *Human Nature and Conduct.* New York: Modern Library.
DiLeonardo, Micaela
1984 *The Varieties of Ethnic Experience.* Ithaca, N.Y.: Cornell University Press.
Dittes, J. E., and H. H. Kelley
1956 "Effects of Different Conditions of Acceptance upon Conformity to Group Norms." *Journal of Abnormal and Social Psychology* 53: 100–107.
Doise, Willem, and G. Mugny
1979 "Individual and Collective Conflicts of Centrations in Cognitive Development." *European Journal of Social Psychology* 9: 105–8
Dubin, Robert
1956 "Industrial Workers' Worlds: A Study of the 'Central Life Interests' of Industrial Workers." *Social Problems* 3: 131–42.
Engels, Friedrich
1926 *The Condition of the Working Class in England in 1844.* London: Allen & Unwin.
Epstein, Cynthia Fuchs
1970 "Encountering the Male Establishment: Sex Status Limits on Women's Careers in the Professions." *American Journal of Sociology* 75: 965–82.
1987 "Multiple Demands and Multiple Roles: The Conditions of Successful Management." In Crosby, ed., 1987: 23–25.
Erikson, Kai
1986 "Work and Alienation." *ASR* 51: 1–8.
Etaux, Claire
1983 "The Influences of Environmental Factors on Sex Differences in Children's Play." In Liss, ed., 1983: 1–19.
Farber, Bernard
1971 *Kinship and Class: A Midwestern Study.* New York: Basic Books.
Fausto-Sterling, Anne
1987 *Myths of Gender: Biological Theories About Women and Men.* New York: Basic Books.
Firth, Raymond
1936 *We, the Tikopia.* London: Allen & Unwin.
Flavell, John
1963 *The Developmental Psychology of Jean Piaget.* Princeton, N.J.: D. Van Nostrand.
Ford, J. V., D. Young, and S. Box
1967 "Functional Autonomy, Role Distance and Social Class." *British Journal of Sociology* 18: 370–81.
Fox, Lynn H., Dianne Tobin, and Linda Brody
1979 "Sex-Role Socialization and Achievement in Mathematics." In Wittig and Petersen, eds., 1979: 303–32.

Freilich, Morris
    1964 "The Natural Triad in Kinship and Complex Systems." *ASR* 29: 529–40.
Freud, Sigmund
    1960 *Jokes and Their Relation to the Unconscious.* London: Hogarth Press and the Institute of Psychoanalysis.
Gilligan, Carol
    1982 *In a Different Voice: Psychological Theory and Women's Development.* Cambridge, Mass.: Harvard University Press.
Glanz, Rudolf
    1976 *The Jewish Woman in America: Two Female Immigrant Generations, 1820–1929.* New York: KTAV Publishing House and National Council of Jewish Women.
Glenn, Evelyn Nakano
    1983 "Split Household, Small Producer and Dual Wage Earner: An Analysis of Chinese-American Family Strategies." *Journal of Marriage and the Family* 45: 35–46.
Gluckman, Max
    1962 "Les rites de passage." In Daryll Forde et al., eds., *Essays on the Ritual of Social Relations.* Manchester: Manchester University Press.
Goffman, Erving
    1955 "On Facework: An Analysis of Ritual Elements in Social Interaction." *Psychiatry* 18: 213–31.
    1961 "Role Distance." In *Encounters.* Indianapolis: Bobbs-Merrill, 85–152.
Goodchild, B.
    1974 "Class Differences in Environmental Perception." *Urban Studies* 11: 157–69.
Goode, William J.
    1960 "A Theory of Role Strain." *ASR* 25: 483–96.
Goody, Esther N.
    1982 *Parenthood and Social Reproduction.* Cambridge, Eng.: Cambridge University Press.
Gouldner, Alvin W.
    1957 "Cosmopolitans and Locals: Toward an Analysis of Latent Social Roles." *Administrative Science Quarterly* 2: 281–306.
Granovetter, Mark
    1973 "The Strength of Weak Ties." *American Journal of Sociology* 78: 1360–80.
    1974 *Getting a Job: A Study of Contacts and Careers.* Cambridge, Mass.: Harvard University Press.
    1982 "The Strength of Weak Ties: A Network Theory Revisited." In Peter V. Marsden and Nan Lin, eds., *Social Structure and Network Analysis.* Beverly Hills, Calif.: Sage, 105–32.

Greenberg, Joanne
1964 *I Never Promised You a Rose Garden.* New York: Holt, Rinehart and Winston.

Greenfield, Patricia Marks, and Jerome S. Bruner
1966 "Culture and Cognitive Growth." *International Journal of Psychology* 1: 89–107.

Grønseth, Erik
1970 "The Dysfunctionality of the Husband Provider Role in Industrialized Societies." Paper for the Seventh World Congress of Sociology.
1971 *The Family in Capitalist Society and the Dysfunctionality of the Husband Provider Role.* Oslo: Instituttet for Sosiologi, mimeo.

Gurin, Patricia
1987 "The Political Implications of Women's Statuses." In Crosby, ed., 1987: 167–98.

Habermas, Jürgen
1979 *Communication and the Evolution of Society.* Boston: Beacon Press.

Hall, Harry S.
1966 "Scientists and Politicians." In Howard M. Vollmer and Donald L. Mills, eds., *Professionalization.* Englewood Cliffs, N.J.: Prentice Hall, 310–21.

Halle, David
1984 *America's Working Man.* Chicago: Chicago University Press.

Hareven, Tamara K.
1982 *Family Time and Industrial Time.* Cambridge, Eng.: Cambridge University Press.

Harris, Lauren Julian
1979 "Sex-Related Differences in Spatial Ability: A Developmental Psychological View." In Kopp and Kirkpatrick, eds., 1979: 133–81.

Henderson, A. M., and Talcott Parsons
1947 "Introduction to Max Weber." In Weber 1947b: 3–86.

Henley, Nancy M.
1985 "Psychology and Gender." *Signs* 11: 101–19.

Hennig, Margaret, and Anne Jardin
1977 *The Management Woman.* Garden City, N.Y.: Anchor.

Henry, Andrew F., and James F. Short, Jr.
1954 *Suicide and Homicide.* Glencoe, Ill.: Free Press.

Henry, Jules
1954 "The Formal Social Structure of a Psychiatric Hospital." *Psychiatry* 17: 139–51.

Hochschild, Arlie, with Anne Machung
1989 *The Second Shift.* New York: Avon Books.

Hollander, E. P.
1958 "Conformity, Status, and Idiosyncrasy Credit." *Psychological Review* 63: 17–27.

180 ·· *Works Cited*

Hollingshead, August B., and Frederick C. Redlich
1958 *Social Class and Mental Illness: A Community Study.* New York: Wiley.
Homans, George C.
1951 *The Human Group.* London: Routledge & Kegan Paul.
Howe, Irving
1976 *World of Our Fathers.* New York: Simon and Schuster.
Hughes, Everett C.
1963 "Professions." *Daedalus* 92: 655–68.
1971a "Dilemmas and Contradictions of Status." In E. Hughes 1971b: 141–50.
1971b *The Sociological Eye: Selected Papers on Institutions and Race.* Chicago: Aldine-Atherton.
Hughes, L.
1977 "The Social Context of Children's Lore in Cooperstown, New York." Master's thesis, State University of New York, Oneonta.
Humphrey, N. K.
1976 "The Social Function of Intellect." In Bateson and Hinde, eds., 1976: 303–17.
Hyde, Janet S.
1981 "How Large Are Cognitive Gender Differences: A Mental Analysis Using Omega (2) and d." *American Psychologist* 36: 892–901.
Hyde, Janet S., E. R. Beiringer, and W. M. Yen
1975 "On the Empirical Relation Between Spatial Ability and Sex Differences in Other Aspects of Cognitive Performance." *Multivariate Behavioral Research* 10: 289–310.
Iglitzin, L. B.
1972 "A Child's Eye View of Sex Roles." *Today's Education* 61: 23–25.
Inhelder, Bärbel, and Jean Piaget
1958 *The Growth of Logical Thinking from Childhood to Adolescence.* New York: Basic Books.
Inkeles, Alex
1984 *Exploring Individual Modernity.* New York: Columbia University Press.
Inkeles, Alex, and David H. Smith
1974 *Becoming Modern.* Cambridge, Mass.: Harvard University Press.
Israel, Joachim
1971 *Alienation from Marx to Modern Sociology.* Boston: Allyn & Bacon.
Jones, Maxwell
1953 *The Therapeutic Community.* New York: Basic Books.
Kagan, Jerome
1972 "A Conception of Early Adolescence." In Kagan and Coles, eds., 1972: 90–105.

Kagan, Jerome, and Robert Coles, eds.
1972 *Twelve to Sixteen: Early Adolescence.* New York: Norton.
Kagan, Jerome, and H. Kogan
1970 "Individuality and Cognitive Performance." In P. H. Mussen, ed., *Carmichael's Manual of Child Psychology.* New York: Wiley.
Kanter, Rosabeth Moss
1968 "Commitment and Social Organization: A Study of Commitment Mechanisms in Utopian Communities." *ASR* 33: 499–517.
Kaplan, Charles P., and Thomas L. Van Valey
1980 "Census '80: Continuing the Factfinder Tradition." Washington, D.C., U.S. Department of Commerce, Bureau of the Census.
Keller, Suzanne
1988 "The American Dream of Community." *Sociological Forum* 3: 167–83.
Kerber, Linda K., Catherine C. Greeno, Eleanor E. Maccoby, Zella Luria, Carol B. Stack, and Carol Gilligan
1986 "On 'In a Different Voice': An Interdisciplinary Forum: Viewpoint." *Signs* 11: 304–33.
Kohlberg, Lawrence, and Carol Gilligan
1972 "The Adolescent as a Philosopher." In Kagan and Coles, eds., 1972: 144–79.
Kohn, Melvin L.
1969a *Class and Conformity: A Study in Values.* Homewood, Ill.: Dorsey Press.
1969b "Social Class and Parent-Child Relationships: An Interpretation." In R. Coser, ed., 1969: 21–42.
1971 "Bureaucratic Man: A Portrait and an Interpretation." *ASR* 36: 461–74.
1975 *Class and Conformity.* Chicago: University of Chicago Press.
1978 "The Reciprocal Effects of the Substantive Complexity of Work and Intellectual Flexibility: A Longitudinal Assessment." *American Journal of Sociology* 84: 24–52.
Kohn, Melvin L., and Carmi Schooler
1973 "Occupational Experience and Psychological Functioning: Assessment of Reciprocal Effects." *ASR* 38: 97–118.
Kohn, Melvin L., and Carmi Schooler, with the collaboration of Jeanne Miller, Karen A. Miller, Carrie Schoenbach, and Ronald Schoenberg
1983 *Work and Personality: An Inquiry into the Impact of Social Stratification.* Norwood, N.J.: Ablex.
Komarovsky, Mirra
1974 "Cultural Contradictions and Sex Roles." In R. Coser, ed., 1974: 512–16.

Kon, Igor S.
  1967 "The Concept of Alienation in Modern Sociology." *Social Research* 34: 507–28.
Kopp, Claire B., and Martha Kirkpatrick, eds.
  1979 *Becoming Female: Perspectives on Development.* New York: Plenum Press.
Kramer, Judith R., and Seymour Leventman
  1961 *Children of the Gilded Ghetto: Three Generations of American Jews.* New Haven, Conn.: Yale University Press.
Ladd, Florence
  1967 "A Note on the World Across the Street." *Harvard Graduate School of Education Association Bulletin* 12: 46–48.
LaGory, Mark, and John Pipkin
  1981 *Urban Social Space.* Belmont, Calif.: Wadsworth.
Lever, Janet
  1976 "Sex Differences in the Games Children Play." *Social Problems* 23: 478–87.
Levi, Carlo
  1947 *Christ Stopped at Eboli: The Story of a Year.* Trans. Frances Frenaye. New York: Farrar, Straus.
Lévi-Strauss, Claude
  1949 *Les Structures Elémentaires de la Parenté.* Paris: Presses Universitaires de France.
Lévy-Bruhl, Lucien
  1966 *How Natives Think.* New York: Washington Square Press.
Liebow, Elliot
  1967 *Tally's Corner.* Boston: Little, Brown.
Linn, Marcia C., and Anne C. Petersen
  1985 "Emergence and Characterization of Sex Differences in Spatial Ability: A Meta-Analysis." *Child Development* 56: 1479–98.
Liss, Marsha B., ed.
  1983 *Social and Cognitive Skills: Sex Roles and Children's Play.* New York: Academic Press.
Litvak, Eugene
  1985 *Helping the Elderly: Complementary Roles of Informal Networks and Formal Systems.* New York: Guilford Press.
Lynch, Kevin, ed.
  1977 *Growing Up in Cities: Studies of the Spatial Environment of Adolescence in Cracow, Melbourne, Mexico City, Salta, Toluca, and Warszawa.* Cambridge, Mass.: MIT Press.
Maccoby, Eleanor
  1963 "Women's Intellect." In Seymour M. Farber and Roger H. L. Wilson, eds., *The Potential of Woman.* New York: McGraw Hill, 24–39.

Maccoby, Eleanor Emmons, and Carol Nagy Jacklin
1974 *The Psychology of Sex Differences.* Stanford, Calif.: Stanford University Press.
Maccoby, Michael, and Nancy Modiano
1966 "On Culture and Equivalence: I." In Bruner et al., eds., 1966: 30–67.
Mannes, Marya
1963 "The Problems of Creative Women." In Seymour M. Farber and Roger H. L. Wilson, eds., *The Potential of Woman.* New York: McGraw Hill, 116–30.
Mannheim, Karl
1951 *Man and Society in an Age of Reconstruction.* London: Routledge and Kegan Paul.
Marcuse, Herbert
1941 *Reason and Revolution.* New York: Oxford University Press.
Marx, Karl
1956 "Economical and Philosophical Manuscripts." In T. B. Bottomore and Maximilien Rubel, eds., *Karl Marx: Selected Writings in Sociology and Social Philosophy.* London: Watts & Co.
1967 *Writings of the Young Marx on Philosophy and Society.* Ed. Lloyd D. Easton and Kurt H. Guddat. Garden City, N.Y.: Doubleday.
Mason, Ward S., Robert J. Dressel, and Robert K. Bain
1959 "Sex Role and the Career Orientation of Beginning Teachers." *Harvard Education Review* 29: 370–83.
McGilligan, R. P.
1971 "Psychological Differentiation, Abilities and Personality." Unpublished doctoral diss., St. Louis University. Cited in Nash 1979.
McPherson, Miller J., and Lynn Smith-Lovin
1982 "Women and Weak Ties: Differences by Sex in the Size of Voluntary Organizations." *American Journal of Sociology* 87: 883–904.
Mead, George Herbert
1946 *Mind, Self, and Society.* Chicago: University of Chicago Press.
Medawar, Peter B.
1976 "Does Ethology Throw Any Light on Human Behavior?" In Bateson and Hinde, eds., 1976: 497–506.
Menzel, Herbert
1957 "Public and Private Conformity Under Different Conditions of Acceptance in the Group." *Journal of Abnormal and Social Psychology* 55: 398–402.
Merton, Robert K.
1949 "Discrimination and the American Creed." In Robert M. MacIver, ed., *Discrimination and National Welfare.* New York: Harper Bros., 99–126.

1957 "Introduction." In R. K. Merton, G. Reader, and P. L. Kendall, eds., *The Student-Physician*. Cambridge, Mass.: Harvard University Press.

1959 "Conformity, Deviation, and Opportunity Structures." *ASR* 24: 177–88.

1968a "Continuities in the Theory of Reference Group Behavior." In Merton 1968d: 422–40.

1968b "Patterns of Influence: Local and Cosmopolitan Influentials." In Merton 1968d: 441–74.

1968c "Social Structure and Anomie." In Merton 1968d: 185–214.

1968d *Social Theory and Social Structure*. New York: Free Press.

Merton, Robert K., and Elinor Barber

1976 "Sociological Ambivalence." In Robert K. Merton, ed., *Sociological Ambivalence and Other Essays*. New York: Free Press, 3–31.

Mesmin, Georges

1973 *L'enfant, l'architecture, et l'espace*. Paris: Casterman.

Mills, Edgar W., Jr.

1982 "Cult Extremism: The Reduction of Normative Dissonance." In Kenneth J. Levi, ed., *Violence and Religious Commitment*. University Park: Penn State University Press, 75–87.

Mugny, Gabriel, Paola DePaolis, and Felice Carugati

1984 "Social Regulations in Cognitive Development." In Willem Doise and Augusto Palmonari, eds., *Social Interaction in Individual Development*. Cambridge, Eng.: Cambridge University Press, 127–46.

Nash, Sharon Churnin

1979 "Sex Role as Mediator of Intellectual Functioning." In Wittig and Petersen, eds., 1979: 263–302.

Nye, Ivan F., and Lois Wladis Hoffman

1963 *The Employed Mother in America*. Chicago: Rand McNally.

Oetzel, R.

1961 "The Relationship Between Sex-Role Acceptance and Cognitive Abilities." Unpublished master's thesis, Stanford University. Cited in Nash 1979.

Orzack, Louis H.

1959 "Work as a 'Central Life Interest' of Professionals." *Social Problems* 7: 125–32.

Papanek, Hanna

1973 "Men, Women, and Work: Reflections on the Two-Person Career." *American Journal of Sociology* 78: 852–72.

Pape, Ruth H.

1964 "Touristry: A Type of Occupational Mobility." *Social Problems* 11: 336–44.

Park, Ezra
1950 *Race and Culture*. Glencoe, Ill.: Free Press.
Parsons, Anne
1969 *Belief, Magic, and Anomie: Essays in Psychosocial Anthropology*. New York: Free Press.
Parsons, Talcott
1949 *The Structure of Social Action*. Glencoe, Ill.: Free Press.
1951 *The Social System*. Glencoe, Ill.: Free Press.
Peel, E. A.
1967 *The Psychological Basis of Education*. Edinburgh: Oliver & Boyd.
Piaget, Jean
1948 *The Moral Judgment of the Child*. Glencoe, Ill.: Free Press.
Powell, Walter W., and Richard Robbins, eds.
1984 *Conflict and Consensus: A Festschrift in Honor of Lewis A. Coser*. New York: Free Press.
Robinson, C. E.
1978 "Sex-Typed Behavior in Children's Spontaneous Play." In *The Association for the Anthropological Study of Play Newsletter*. Champaign: University of Illinois Children's Research Center, 14–17.
Rosenberg, Florence R., and Roberta G. Simmons
1975 "Sex Differences in the Self-Concept in Adolescence." *Sex Roles* 1: 147–59.
Rossi, Alice S.
1964 "Equality Between the Sexes: An Immodest Proposal." *Daedalus* 93: 607–57.
1965 "Barriers to the Career Choice of Engineering, Medicine, or Science Among American Women." In J. A. Mattfeld and C. E. Van Aken, eds., *Women and the Scientific Professions*. Cambridge, Mass.: MIT Press, 51–127.
Rossi, Joseph A.
1983 "Ratios Exaggerate Gender Differences in Mathematical Ability." *American Psychologist* 38: 348.
Schooler, Carmi
1984 "Psychological Effects of Complex Environments During the Life Span: A Review and Theory." *Intelligence* 8: 259–81.
Scribner, Sylvia, and Michael Cole
1973 "Cognitive Consequences of Formal and Informal Education." *Science* 182: 553–59.
Seeman, Melvin
1959 "On the Meaning of Alienation." *ASR* 24: 783–91.
Sherman, Julia A.
1967 "Problem of Sex Differences in Space Perception and Aspects of Intellectual Functioning." *Psychological Review* 74: 290–99.

1982 "Mathematics the Critical Filter: A Look at Some Residues." *Psychology of Women Quarterly*: 428–44.

Sieber, Sam D.
1974 "Toward a Theory of Role Accumulation." *ASR* 39: 567–78.

Simmel, Georg
1950 *The Sociology of Georg Simmel*. Trans. Kurt Wolff. Glencoe, Ill.: Free Press.
1955 "The Web of Group Affiliations." In *Conflict and the Web of Group Affiliations*. Trans. Kurt H. Wolff and Reinhard Bendix. New York: Free Press.

Slater, Philip
1974 "Social Limitations on Libidinal Withdrawal." In R. Coser, ed., 1974: 111–33.

Snoek, Diedrick J.
1966 "Role Strain in Diversified Role-Sets." *American Journal of Sociology* 71: 363–72.

Spitz, Rene A., and Katherine M. Wolf
1946 "Anaclitic Depression: An Inquiry into the Genesis of the Psychiatric Conditions in Early Childhood." *Psychoanalytic Study of the Child* 2: 313–42.

Sprafkin, Carol, et al.
1983 "Sex-Differentiated Play: Cognitive Consequences and Early Interventions." In Liss, ed., 1983: 167–92.

Stacey, Judith
1983 *Patriarchy and Socialist Revolution in China*. Berkeley: University of California Press.

Stack, Carol
1974 *All Our Kin*. New York: Harper & Row.

Stanley, Julian C., and Camilla P. Benbow
1982 "Huge Sex Ratios at Upper End." *American Psychologist* 27: 972.

Stevenson, Harold W., and Richard S. Newman
1985 "Long-Term Prediction of Achievement and Attitudes in Mathematics and Reading." Unpublished manuscript.

Stinchcombe, Arthur L.
1975 "Merton's Theory of Social Structure." In L. Coser, ed., 1975: 11–33.

Streufert, Siegfried, and Susan C. Streufert
1978 *Behavior in the Complex Environment*. New York: Wiley.

Strotzka, Hans
1969 "Zur Psychosozialen Lage Berufstaetiger Frauen." In Leopold Rosenmayr and Sigrud Hoellinger, eds., *Sozialforschung in Oesterreich*. Vienna: Verlag Herrman Boehlaus Nachf, 543–58.

Sutton-Smith, Brian
1979 "The Play of Girls." In Kopp and Kirkpatrick, eds., 1979: 229–57.

Swanson, Guy
1960 *The Birth of the Gods*. Ann Arbor: University of Michigan Press.
Tanner, J. M., and B. Inhelder, eds.
1958 *Discussions on Child Development*. New York: International Universities Press.
Toennies, Ferdinand
1887 *Gemeinschaft und Gesellschaft*. Leipzig: Fues's Verlag.
Tolstoy, Leo
1960 "The Death of Ivan Illich." In *The Death of Ivan Illich and Other Stories*. New York: Signet Books, 110–16.
Turner, Ralph
1962 "Role Taking: Process Versus Conformity." In Arnold M. Rose, ed., *Human Behavior and Social Processes*. Boston: Houghton Mifflin, 220–40.
Turner, Ralph, and Lewis M. Killian
1972 *Collective Behavior*. Englewood, N.J.: Prentice Hall.
Vygotsky, L. S.
1962 *Thought and Language*. Cambridge, Mass.: MIT Press.
Ward, Colin
1978 *The Child in the City*. New York: Pantheon Books.
Weber, Max
1947a *From Max Weber: Essays in Sociology*. Ed. H. H. Gerth and C. Wright Mills. London: Routledge & Kegan Paul.
1947b *The Theory of Social and Economic Organization*. Trans. M. Henderson and Talcott Parsons. New York: Oxford University Press.
1978 *Economy and Society*. Ed. Guenther Roth and Claus Wittich. Berkeley: University of California Press.
Whyte, William Foote
1943 *Street Corner Society*. Chicago: University of Chicago Press.
1951 "Small Groups and Large Organizations." In J. Rohrer and M. Sherif, eds., *Social Psychology at the Crossroads*. New York: Harper Bros., 297–312.
Witkin, H. A., R. B. Dyk, H. F. Faterson, D. R. Goodenogh, and S. A. Karp
1962 *Psychological Differentiation*. New York: Wiley.
Wittig, Michele Andrisin
1976 "Sex Differences in Intellectual Functioning: How Much of a Difference Do Genes Make?" *Sex Roles* 2: 63–74.
Wittig, Michele Andrisin, and Anne C. Petersen, eds.
1979 *Sex-Related Differences in Cognitive Functioning*. New York: Academic Press.
Woolf, Virginia
1929 *A Room of One's Own*. New York: Harcourt Brace Jovanovich.

NAME INDEX

In this index an "f" after a number indicates a separate reference on the next page, and an "ff" indicates separate references on the next two pages. A continuous discussion over two or more pages is indicated by a span of page numbers, e.g., "57–59." *Passim* is used for a cluster of references in close but not consecutive sequence.

SUBJECT INDEX

In this index an "f" after a number indicates a separate reference on the next page, and an "ff" indicates separate references on the next two pages. A continuous discussion over two or more pages is indicated by a span of page numbers, e.g., "57–59." *Passim* is used for a cluster of references in close but not consecutive sequence.

Abstractness, 146f, 163. *See also* Cognitive development; Formal operational thinking

Activity system, *see* Role-set

Adaptation, *see* Adjustment; Intellectual flexibility; Work flexibility

Adjustment, 4, 76, 96–97. *See also* Intellectual flexibility; Work flexibility

Adolescence, 4, 145–56

Alienation: multirelational synchronization and, 18–19, 21–22; role-set complexity and, 26, 35; conditions for individuation and, 26; as term, 31; isolation and, 34, 54; as psychological state, 34; in work situation, 51f; structural determinants of, 60

Allegiances, 113–15, 123–24, 127–29, 149. *See also* Cultural mandate for women; Expectations, contradictory

Anomie, *see* Alienation; Isolation

Attitudes, *see* Conformity, behavioral vs. attitudinal; Internal dispositions; Work

Authority structure, 40–44, 94–96

Automation, 36–37, 46

Autonomy, 168

Behavior, *see* Conformity, behavioral vs. attitudinal

Boundaries, and individuation, 91–93

Bridge between relationships, 79, 108

Bureaucracy, 34–35, 38–39

Career choices: for women, 120–23, 134–35, 163–64; adolescents and, 146–50 *passim*, 161

Celibacy, and greedy institutions, 73

Centrifugality, vs. centripetality, 97–98

Ceremonies, 4

sets and, 22, 45, 63–64, 156–57; role articulation and, 23–25, 46, 65f, 101; nurses and, 41; interprofessional conflict and, 61; empathy and, 67; status articulation and, 118; college women and, 135
Externality, 106. *See also* Ties, strong vs. weak

Family: role segmentation and, 2, 27, 94–97; as gemeinschaft, 75–76, 94, 137–39; as greedy institution, 94, 110, 123, 138; socialization and, 96–97, 108; centrifugal vs. centripetal, 97–98; disruptions caused by, 113f, 117–19, 123–25, 130–32; allegiance of women to, 123–24, 127–29, 149. *See also* Cultural mandate for women; Immigrant families
Family structure, types of, 97–105
Field independence, 141–42, 163
Flexibility, *see* Intellectual flexibility; Work flexibility
Formal operational thinking, 12–13, 147
Foster parenting, 106f

Games, 152–56, 164; definition of, 153. *See also* Team sports
Gemeinschaft: role articulation and, 26; cognitive development and, 26–27, 139–40; concept of, 31, 71–73; powerlessness and, 36; hostility in, 59, 90; conflict in, 72, 90; greedy institutions and, 73–75; family as, 75–76, 94, 137–39; modern society and, 75–77; dialect and, 87–88; opportunity and, 88–89; social control in, 91; strong vs. weak ties in, 98–105; use of space and, 137–39; as disempowering, 168. *See also*

Family; Particularistic vs. universalistic relationships; Simple role-set
Gender differences, 136–50 *passim*
Genevans, 157
Geriatric patients, 38
German-Jewish Americans, 99–102
Gesellschaft, 31f, 76
Goal definition, 61–62, 65–66
Godfather, 108
Greedy institution, 73–75, 79f, 110, 123, 138. *See also* Family; Gemeinschaft
Group, close vs. loosely structured, 90

Helping, *see* Claim structure
Het Nieuwsblad, 75–76
Hilltown, 59–60
Homicide rates, vs. suicide rates, 72n
Hospitals: patient role-sets in, 37–38; role-sets for personnel in, 40–45; understaffing in, 56–59. *See also* Medicine; Nurses
Humor, 7
Hutterite communities, 90–91

Idiosyncracy credit, 131
Immigrant families, 14–15, 97–105
Inanimate objects, 82
Individualism, 11–12, 32–33, 91–93
Individuation, 20–22, 25–26, 169
Industrialization, 15–16, 52
Industry, 34–35, 36–37, 45–46
Innovation, 44–45, 66–67. *See also* Intellectual flexibility
Intellectual flexibility: acquisition of, 10–11; social structure and, 13, 14–15, 66f, 157; bureaucracy and, 34–35; powerlessness and, 168. *See also* Cognitive development

99–105; socioeconomic status and, 101–3; women's access to, 120, 123–25; for individuation, 169

"Organic solidarity," 60

Overcommitment, 90

Overconformity, 132–33

Pakistan, family in, 75–76

Particularistic vs. universalistic relationships, 77–85, 154–55

Personal identity, 37, 52–53, 149. *See also* Individuation

Physical space, use of, 137–39, 142–45, 159–62f

"Plurality of life worlds," 18, 21. *See also* Role-set complexity

Politics, 105

Poverty, 168

Power, 47; of role partners, 23; role-set complexity and, 42, 43–44

Powerlessness, 35–36, 62, 168

Pre-industrial society, 15–16, 95–96

Prestige, 120–21f, 126, 128–29

Primitive logic, 85–86

Professions: conflict within, 59, 60–61; self-image and, 64–66; commitment and, 114, 127–29; unequal representation of women in, 123; solidarity within, 127; women-dominated, status of, 129

Psychotherapy, 84

Public anxiety, and women's roles, 120, 134–35

Reciprocity, 79–80

Reisefieber, 5

Relational system, *see* Role-set

Relativity, sense of, 9–13

Replaceability, 124, 125–29

Restricted role-set, *see* Simple role-set

Ritualism, 40, 44–45, 50. *See also* Routinization

Role articulation, 1–5; individuation and, 20–22; role segmentation as source of, 21–22; status articulation and, 22–23; mechanisms for, 23–25, 46, 66, 116–17; opportunity structure and, 46–47; inclusive vs. noninclusive roles and, 53–54; collective activity and, 64–66; role-set complexity and, 88; for women vs. men, 113, 117; normative priorities and, 116–17, 119–20

Role partners, 23, 38, 89. *See also* Expectations, contradictory; Role-set complexity

Role-playing, 92

Role segmentation: family and, 2, 27, 94–97; child development and, 7–13; socialization and, 7–13, 96–97; social conditions and, 14; industrialization and, 15–16; notion of, 19; implications of, 19–23; alienation and, 32; individualism and, 32–33; formal education and, 83–84; gender differences in, 157–58; bonding and, 169

Role-set, as term, 20, 115

Role-set complexity, 22, 25, 32n; cognitive capabilities and, 14–15, 156–59; alienation and, 26, 35; social hierarchy and, 32–33; in medical vs. surgical hospital wards, 40–45; work dissatisfaction and, 50–51; adolescent differences in, 150–56; gender differences in, over life cycle, 160–61. *See also* Complex role-set; Simple role-set

Routinization, 114–17, 126–27. *See also* Ritualism

Library of Congress Cataloging-in-Publication Data

Coser, Rose Laub, 1916–
  In defense of modernity : role complexity and individual autonomy
/ Rose Laub Coser.
   p. cm.
  Includes bibliographical references (p.   ) and index.
  ISBN 0-8047-1871-7
  1. Social role. 2. Autonomy (Psychology) 3. Alienation (Social
psychology) 4. Gemeinschaft and gesellschaft (Sociology)
I. Title.
HM131.C74775 1991
302.5′44—dc20   91-6374
                                                      CIP

∞ This book is printed on acid-free paper